You Deserve...
HEALTH, HAPPINESS, SUCCESS, PROSPERITY, & LOVE!

JOAN B TOWNSEND

Print ISBN: 978-1-54398-544-3

eBook ISBN: 978-1-54398-545-0

ACKNOWLEDGMENTS

God has granted me the opportunity to meet people from all walks of life and from all over the world and everyone has a story! I have listened to interesting conversations, eloquent preaching, spectacular teaching and read conscious enlightening books and/or letters that have been intentionally written with care and purpose. Therefore, I dedicate this book to all of those sages, teachers, preachers, friends, family, the very young and the very old, those that are living and those that have transitioned on and to offer privacy names have been changed and/or omitted and any events that resembles an occurrence that you have experienced is purely coincidental.

However, for the following people you have been most valuable to me as your words were infectious and has helped to change my perception of life for the better: Dr. Hassan, M.D., Dr. Goode, M.D., Albert Greene, Dr. K.C. Price, Bishop T. D. Jakes, Rev. Michael B. Beckwith, Rev. Frederick J. Eikerenkoetter II, Dr. Wayne Dyer PhD, Shawn C. Carter, Persian Poet Rumi, and The Holy Bible (King James Version).

Eternal love,

Joan B. Townsend

You

Deserve…

1

Deserving is one of life's concepts that so many people shy away from because it speaks to their subconscious minds and to their heart of hearts that they are worthy to be treated in a way that will esteems them higher than their conscious minds allows them to think about themselves. This pre-conditioning thought process of being not deserving enough is often times a result of environmental conditioning originating from generational curses passed on either consciously or subconsciously from generation to generation or from the neighborhood you grew up in or the golf team you belonged to. There are so many different situation and circumstances that affect the way we think about ourselves as well as about others. Some cultures conditions their people to think because they are born in a particular family that they can never rise above that families economic, educational, health and welfare in life. Meaning if you were born to parents that are servants then you'll become a servant. After all that was what your great grandfather did, your grandfather, and your father so it's only right that you too will be a servant. Wrong!!! We all deserve to be and to do whatever we desire to do and be in this game called life. Therefore, breaking the concept that you must fall in line with the generational curse of poverty, lack, hopelessness is erroneous to the infinite degree! Delete the concept that have been deep-rooted in your mind to think that you are unworthy of life's many delicious and most auspicious rewards that so many people are able to take for granted all because they've been taught that they deserve the best and only the best all of the time.

For this reason, I asked myself the question of why is it that some people "buy in" to not enough shying away from the goodness of life and some people accept and expect the goodness of life and will have it no other way! Or better yet, why is it that some people are taught from birth that they deserve the best and are born into an environment where all that they see are the wonderful things in and of life. When on the other hand, another baby born at the same exact time to parents that live in abstract poverty and the baby grows up seeing the struggles and strife of life and low and behold I had my answer. One child has wealth, love, happiness instilled within them from conception. The couple find out they are pregnant and are over joyed and throw a "baby having" party! On the other hand the other couple finds out they are pregnant and are overwhelmed with grief of how will they be able to afford all of the items that come along with being pregnant and birthing a baby into the world. Stress immediately sets in with the mother and unborn child regarding what their fate in life will be.

Armed with an innate curiosity I began talking to people about everything that life could offer be the experience positive, negative, or indifferent. It really didn't make a difference to me about color, creed, nationality, income levels, or if they were green with polka dot stripes, glowed in the moonlight or hid from the daylight. If you had a story to tell and everyone does I had ears and made time to hear that story. I became interested in the game of life and all of its players and for the first time the old saying of "don't have the player hate the game" meant more to me than simply being something cool I learned to say way back in junior high school.

Suddenly, God graciously opened up the windows of His Universe and began to bring people from every nationality, economic status, religious preference,

Centennials to Baby-boomers from all across the globe into my space of time and place to talk to me about the things that matter most to them or things that they cared most about. I had strangers opening up to talk to me in the most unusual places. One time I listened to a young man talk to me about his wife, children, and her boyfriend in a mobile phone store for 2 hours and when he finished talking he looked at me and apologized for talking to me for so long especially since he didn't know me. I smiled and assured him that it was okay, because obviously he needed someone to talk to. Before long every time I went somewhere I ran into people that wanted to talk to me about music, cars, vacations, suicide, careers, jobs, children, relationships, prison, clothes, housing, finances, celebrities, food, sex, water, health, dis-eases, sports, movies, birthdays, parents, friends, co-workers, hurts, pains, disappointments, organ donations, religion, God, Mother Earth, parallel planets, Atlas Shrugging, genetics, murder, presidential elections, burning of cares, skin color, ultra-violet rays, suga daddies, tattoos, juicing, motor cycles, and so much more! I felt as if God was speaking through me to His children, because more often than not when the conversation would be over I'd walk away saying "God I know that was you, because I don't know a thing about that" or "Lord thank you for being there, because s/he needed you today and I did too, because I wouldn't have known what to say or how to act to that conversation on my own". Before long I had transitioned from a struggling participant over to a willing participant allowing the love of God to demonstrate through me.

Please keep in mind that the people that came across my path were so diverse in cultures that I was amazed to realize that each human experience regardless of the package it was being delivered from was like a red onion strong enough to make you cry from the many layers of unfortunate bitter issues to the sweetness of the juices of freedom once enough layers were peeled back enough to release the benefits of going through the sting of the situation. I began to understand that the cares were the same regardless of fame, fortune, gender, sexual, bisexual, no sexual, try sexual, pink skin, brown skin, long hair, no hair, educated, saint, sinner, American, Russian, it really didn't matter and that most differences resided in the minds of the individuals that thought that she or he was different in some way.

It was interesting to recognize the emotions and mind sets of those that gave no thought to deserving to be healthy, happy, successful, prosperous, experiencing unconditional love and money to the emotions and mind sets of those that worried about and even subconsciously and sometimes consciously thought that they did not deserve to be healthy, happy, successful, prosperous, experiencing unconditional love, and money. As I continued to ponder why the difference in some people and even figuring out where I myself stood on each topic I succumbed to the ideology of 'this is my view for right now until this view is proven that it no longer serves me then, and only then, will I be mature enough to let this view go and evolve to a more enlightened view of the subject matter at hand and that it will be okay if I changed my mind for the sake of growth and evolution'. I realized it was going to be an interesting journey to discovering answers that are hidden in plain sight as well as hidden answers to questions that even the persons that they are hidden from don't recognize are hidden from them!

Case in point, a happy go lucky Caucasian thirty something lady in Virginia named Ginna had brown hair, a big smile and freckles was having a light hearted conversation with me about her work environment and she told me that there will always be "worker bees" and that all of the ladies in her office that did the bulk of the work but paid the least wages were African American women and that it will always be that way. Ginna felt deserving of a higher salary for doing the least amount of work and she enjoyed the thought of being paid more than the African American women that were hard at work shuffling papers and crunching numbers on a computer all day. Interested in this point of view I then talked to one of the African American women in Ginna's office curious to hear how they felt about working in a Ginnaism environment. Upon approaching one of the African American women, I immediately noticed the lack of luster and enthusiasm that I noticed in Ginna and I casually began the con-versation just as Ginna had began the conversation with me and I asked her view on the work to salary difference and her response was "girl, I'm just happy to have a job I keep my head down and do what they ask me to do, collect my check and gone on about my business, besides they give raises to who they want to when they want to". Pausing for a few moments to size me up she continued with "you know these white folks think they are better than everybody else".

Intrigued by the differences of perceptions the two ladies carried in their hearts one of deserving and one of acceptance I thought about the two babies mentioned above one born into the concept of deserving by loving parents and one born into an environment of struggle and defeatism of wondering if survival is possible. I kept thinking about the statements and ideologies of "there will always be worker bees" and "you know these people think they are better than everybody else". Later that night I asked God to give me answers to why one ladies view point was one of deserving and the other ladies view point was that of defeatism. I began aimlessly looking through papers, pictures, letters, and post cards that I had received over the years from various people not looking for anything in particular, but just looking and smiling as I came across certain tokens that brought back memories and smiles. I picked up two old warn letters that a man named John Brown had given to me when I was about 10 years old that I had read and knew there was value in the letters that John Brown had given to me as he always had a lesson of some sort to teach me. The first letter was written by Willie Lynch and the second letter was written by Jourdon Anderson:

Greetings,

Gentlemen. I greet you here on the bank of the James River in the year of our Lord one thousand seven hundred and twelve. First, I shall thank you, the gentlemen of the Colony of Virginia, for bringing me here. I am here to help you solve some of your problems with slaves. Your invitation reached me on my modest plantation in the West Indies, where I have experimented with some of the newest, and still the oldest, methods for control of slaves. Ancient Rome would envy us if my program is implemented. As our boat sailed south on the James River, named for our illustrious King, whose version of the Bible we cherish, I saw enough to know that your problem is not unique. While Rome used cords of wood as crosses for standing human bodies along its highways in great numbers, you are here using the tree and the rope on occasions. I caught the whiff of a dead slave hanging from a tree, a couple miles back. You are not only losing valuable stock by hangings, you are having upris- ings, slaves are running away, your crops are sometimes left in the fields too long for max- imum profit, you suffer occasional fires, your animals are killed. Gentlemen, you know what your problems are; I do not need to elaborate. I am not here to enumerate your problems, I am here to introduce you to a method of solving them. In my bag here, I HAVE A FULL PROOF METHOD FOR CONTROLLING YOUR BLACK SLAVES. I guarantee every one of you that, if installed correctly, IT WILL CONTROL THE SLAVES FOR AT LEAST 300 HUNDREDS YEARS. My method is simple. Any mem- ber of your family or your overseer can use it. I HAVE OUTLINED A NUMBER OF DIFFERENCES AMONG THE SLAVES; AND I TAKE THESE DIFFERENCES AND MAKE THEM BIGGER. I USE FEAR, DISTRUST AND ENVY FOR CONTROL PURPOSES. These methods have worked on my modest plantation in the West Indies and it will work throughout the South. Take this simple little list of differences and think about them. On top of my list is "AGE," but it's there only because it starts with an "a." The second is "COLOR" or shade. There is INTELLIGENCE, SIZE, SEX, SIZES OF PLANTATIONS, STATUS on plantations, ATTITUDE of owners, whether the slaves live in the valley, on a hill, East, West, North, South, have fine hair, course hair, or is tall or short. Now that you have a list of differences, I shall give you an outline of action, but before that, I shall assure you that DISTRUST IS STRONGER THAN TRUST AND ENVY STRONGER THAN ADULATION, RESPECT OR ADMIRATION. The Black slaves after receiving this indoctrination shall carry on and will become self-refueling and self-generating for HUNDREDS of years, maybe THOUSANDS. Don't forget, you must pitch the OLD black male vs. the YOUNG black male, and the YOUNG black male against the OLD black male. You must use the DARK skin slaves vs. the LIGHT skin slaves, and the LIGHT skin slaves vs. the DARK skin slaves. You must use the FEMALE vs. the MALE, and the MALE vs. the FEMALE. You must also have white servants and overseers [who] distrust all Blacks. But it is NECESSARY THAT YOUR SLAVES TRUST AND DEPEND ON US. THEY MUST LOVE, RESPECT AND TRUST ONLY US. Gentlemen, these kits are your keys to control. Use them. Have your wives and children use them, never miss an opportunity. IF USED INTENSELY FOR ONE YEAR, THE SLAVES THEMSELVES WILL REMAIN PERPETUALLY DISTRUSTFUL. Thank you gentlemen."

Dayton, Ohio,

August 7, 1865

To My Old Master, Colonel P.H.
Anderson, Big Spring, Tennessee

Sir: I got your letter, and was glad to
find that you had not forgotten Jourdon,
and that you wanted me to come back and
live with you again, promising to do better
for me than anybody else can. I have often
felt uneasy about you. I thought the Yankees
would have hung you long before this, for
harboring Rebs they found at your house. I
suppose they never heard about your going
to Colonel Martin's to kill the Union soldier
that was left by his company in their stable.
Although you shot at me twice before I left
you, I did not want to hear of your being
hurt, and am glad you are still living. It would
do me good to go back to the dear old home
again, and see Miss Mary and Miss Martha
and Allen, Esther, Green, and Lee. Give my

love to them all, and tell them I hope we will meet in the better world, if not in this. I would have gone back to see you all when I was working in the Nashville Hospital, but one of the neighbors told me that Henry intended to shoot me if he ever got a chance.

I want to know particularly what the good chance is you propose to give me. I am doing tolerably well here. I get twenty-five dollars a month, with victuals and clothing; have a comfortable home for Mandy,—the folks call her Mrs. Anderson,—and the children—Milly, Jane, and Grundy—go to school and are learning well. The teacher says Grundy has a head for a preacher. They go to Sunday school, and Mandy and me attend church regularly. We are kindly treated. Sometimes we overhear others saying, "Them colored people were slaves" down in Tennessee. The children feel hurt when they hear such remarks; but I tell them it was no disgrace in Tennessee to belong to Colonel Anderson. Many darkeys would have been proud, as I used to be, to call you master. Now if you will write and say what wages you will give me, I will be better able to decide whether it would be to my advantage to move back again.

As to my freedom, which you say I can have, there is nothing to be gained on that score, as I got my free papers in 1864 from the Provost-Marshal-General of the Department of Nashville. Mandy says she would be afraid to go back without some proof that you were disposed to treat us justly and kindly; and we have concluded to test your sincerity by asking you to send us our wages for the time we served you. This will make us forget and forgive old scores, and rely on your justice and friendship in the future. I served you faithfully for thirty-two years, and Mandy twenty years. At twenty-five dollars a month for me, and two dollars a week for Mandy, our earnings would amount to eleven thousand six hundred and eighty dollars. Add to this the interest for the time our wages have been kept back, and deduct what you paid for our clothing, and three doctor's visits to me, and pulling a tooth for Mandy, and the balance will show what we are in justice entitled to. Please send the money by Adams's Express, in care of V. Winters, Esq., Dayton, Ohio. If you fail to pay us for faithful labors in the past, we can have little faith in your promises in the future. We trust the good Maker has opened your eyes to the wrongs which you and your fathers have done to me and my fathers, in making us toil for you for generations without recompense. Here I draw my wages every Saturday night; but in Tennessee there was never any pay-day for the negroes any more than for the horses and cows. Surely there will be a day of reckoning for those who defraud the laborer of his hire.

In answering this letter, please state if there would be any safety for my Milly and Jane, who are now grown up, and both good-looking girls. You know how it was with poor Matilda and Catherine. I would rather stay here and starve—and die, if it come to that—than have my girls brought to shame by the violence and wickedness of their young masters. You will also please state if there has been any schools opened for the colored children in your neighborhood. The great desire of my life now is to give my children an education, and have them form virtuous habits.

Say howdy to George Carter, and thank him for taking the pistol from you when you were shooting at me.

From your old servant,

Jourdon Anderson.

This is why it is very important that the term "deserve" is explained. I want you to know that it is acceptable to deserve more or to deserve better than what you already have. In fact, I'm going so far as to say it is required! It is okay for you to enjoy all of the goodness of life experiencing more than what you currently have and better than what you currently have with no apologies for desiring more or better after all it is your inheritance as a child of God and for being born into this world that you deserve all of the goodness of life! After all 3 John 1:2 teaches us by saying "Beloved, I wish above all things that thou mayest prosper and be in health, even as thy soul prospereth. If more or better is available then you should have it to enjoy what would be a fulfilling life for you after all isn't that is why more or better was created? God put it in somebody's mind to create the very thing that you desire and He put in your heart to desire the very thing that you want. You can have 'things' just don't let the 'things' have you! God wants you to think, know, and feel that you deserve to have all of the goodness of life. The 23rd Psalm says "The Lord is my shepherd; I shall not want" and Acts 10:34, 35 (KJV) teaches us that God is no respecter of persons but in every nation he that feareth him, and worketh righteousness is accepted with him. Therefore, it doesn't matter to whom you were born to You Deserve the best that this earth has to offer and that according to your faith be it unto you Matthew 9:29 (KJV). According to the Caucasian lady the African American employees were "worker bees" and according to the African American lady she was going to "keep her head down" which gives credence to Numbers 13:33 (KJV) and there we saw the giants, the sons of Anak, which come of the giants: and we were in our own sight as grasshoppers (or worker bees), and so we were in their sight. How do you see yourself? How do you treat yourself? Are you defeated before you ever play in the game? Do you not know that people will treat you the way you treat yourself? While you are praying for someone else to be blessed have you thought about praying for yourself to be blessed? This isn't selfishness it is unselfishness! Jourdon wanted only good things for his former slave master was he wrong for wanting only good things for himself?

This is the unfortunate situations that some unsuspecting people have submitted to without knowing the reasons behind the behavior. They have been taught to think, act, be, do what they are acting, being, doing with no hesitations or reservations just be happy with any kind of treatment be it ill will or not and be happy just to have a job! As a result, a full complete healthy joyful life of total fulfillment has been side stepped to accept just enough to get by mentalities with years of broken and or unfulfilled dreams and some have placed this mentality of "accepting" on to their children and their grandchildren for up to possibly 1,000 generations (according to Willie Lynch) to come instead of instilling into them the concept of deserving. The desire to be better, do better, think better, speak better, act better, and feeling better, hey after all You Deserve to enjoy the astonishing things of life! One can only teach what they themselves have been taught so consider this: what have you been taught? Whereas, some people have instilled the mentality of "deserving" on to their children for generations to up to 1,000 generations to come and of course these mindsets will depend on who you are talking to. People get into a never ending cycle of low expectations or in some cases no expectations with emotions of undeserving attitudes when others are happily enjoying the goodness of life knowing, feeling, and believing that they deserve to be happy through and through without a question of a doubt!

Know what you want and "feel" it as if you already have it is a Biblical principle taught by father, Abraham; which is a generational lesson passed on from one father to another father. You know the saying: Abraham, Isaac, and Jacob but it should have been Abraham, Isaac, and Esau ~~~ anyway! So you are thinking you didn't have an earthly father to teach you this principle no worries you are learning it now! All is well! Father, Abraham; wanted a son to leave as heir to all that he had and he didn't want to leave one of his servants as his heir. He asked for an heir and God's response is according to Romans 4:17 (KJV) (As it is written, I have made thee a father of many nations,) before him whom he believed, even God, who quickeneth the dead for Abraham was an old man wanting to have a son, and God calleth those things which be not as though they were. Abraham had to realize this promise through faith at the time of the promise because he was up in age and he had no children at all at the time of the promise! How was he going to be the father of many nations when neither his equipment nor his wife's equipment are working? He had to realize the promise through faith ~ that's how! Through faith of taking God at His word and feeling deserving simply because he was God's child he had to believe on trust in God's Words and at one hundred years of age Isaac was born!!! Also, just a little extra information about the situation Sarah, Abraham's wife, interfered with God's plans for Abraham's first born son to be born and to this day there are still issues in certain parts of the world as a result of Sarah taking things into her own hands and interfering with thus says the Lord! Now when God decree and declare a thing my advice to you is stay out of it and let God do what He does and if you don't know the story you'll have to read it for yourself in order to get all of the business on that back in the day baby momma drama! Well guess what you are God's child, too, and You Deserve to have the best in this life so do not let a Sarah (other people's opinions) of where you were born, the color of your skin, your age, or any other issue interfere with you receiving and accepting your blessings from the Source of Creation! Think and feel that you deserve to be blessed!

Now if you have never been told this before then allow me to be the first to say or to reiterate to you that You Deserve the best out of life! Now, take heed to these words, because I can only tell you this amazing truth about your deservability of life's best of the best now you have to do your part and know that you deserve the best! You have to feel that you deserve the best! You have to believe within your inner most depth of belief that you deserve the absolute best! You can be whatever you want to be! You can do whatever you want to do! You can have whatever you want to have without taking anything from anyone else! The choice is yours you can get with up or down, wrong or right, deserving or undeserving! You decide! You make the decision! The choice is yours! Genesis 27:21(KJV) explains it this way by telling of a story of a blessing being given to what has been said to be the wrong son, but in actuality the blessing is given to anyone that feels the she or he deserves to be blessed! The story tells us that the father was getting ready to transition from this world on to the next dimension and wanted to pass the blessings of this world on to his eldest son which was the custom in those days. The eldest son that was supposedly deserving of the blessing was hairy and the younger son was smooth. The mother knowing that the father was ready to pass on the blessing to the oldest son told the younger son whom she favored that she would dress him like his brother, the eldest son, so that he could go in to the father's tent to receive his brother's blessings while the elder brother was out hunting. Isaac, the father, said unto Jacob (the younger son), come near, I pray thee, that I may feel thee, my son, whether thou be my very son Esau (eldest son) or not. You have to understand that Isaac, the father, was blind and had to feel the son and smell the son to see if he was the right son or not and God like blind Isaac want to feel our emotions, our intentions to decide if we are deserving of the blessings or not! God do not want us to give lip service, because he knows talk can be one of the cheapest commodities ever with the mouth being full of cursings, deceit, and fraud! Under the tongue is mischief and vanity Psalm 10:7 and of course the teachings of Proverbs 18:21 teaches us that death and life are in the power of the tongue: and they that love it shall eat the fruit thereof. Therefore, keep forever in your remembrance that God wants to know how you feel about a situation or circumstance, because those emotions/feelings that lie in what you think is a dormant status on the inside manifest what you see on the outside. God understands that people will say anything, but the sincerity of their emotions cannot be concealed. I pray this day that you choose to change your mind and change your emotions as it is okay to have a changed mind and emotions and please understand that according to your faith be it unto you Matthew 9:29 (KJV). Take God at His Word don't be like Sarah!

Now, focus your attention on the Father being blind and desiring to feel you instead of looking at your outer appearance. The Father's concern wasn't what the son looked like, but what he felt like! Do you feel like you deserve to be blessed? When the Father calls you into Him (and please believe me He will summons you) will you feel like you deserve to be blessed? Will you smell like you deserve to be blessed? Understand that the Father is blind to whom you were born to; what country you came from; and what you look like! You can be pink, brown, yellow, red, black, striped, polka dots, spotted, tall, short, and all aspects in between it really doesn't make a difference if the Father wants you blessed then consider yourself blessed. The Father doesn't care what you look like He is blind to your looks! The Father cares about what you feel like! I'll say this again: do you feel like you deserve to be blessed? Stop considering your outer appearance considering what you look like and deciding on what you look like in someone else's eyes (we were grasshoppers in our eyes so we look like grasshoppers in their eyes)! Other people are going to see whatever it is that you see about you! They are going to treat you like you treat you! Perhaps, according to all outer appearances and circumstances you were born to the wrong parents, on the wrong side of town, wrapped in the wrong color skin, and according to society you are not the right person that is deserving of the blessings according to all of the circumstantial evidence. But if you can feel like you deserve the blessings to the point of the feelings emitting a sweet smelling fragrance to the Father that you are deserving what you have come to receive then you will receive the Father's blessings! The Father is blind to the customs of the times and to all of the circumstantial evidence indicating that you are the wrong person to receive His blessings. The Father is blind to what you look like so stop looking at the evidence of what you are and where you are and start looking at Whose you are! The Father cares about what you feel like and I can't say that enough! How are you feeling?! O'shea Jackson gave out some very accurate advice when he told everyone to "check yourself before you wreck yourself" and ladies and gentlemen; boys and girls I'm sincere when I ask "how do you feel?" You've got to get your emotions in check in knowing that You Deserve the best! Gone are the days of "accepting" and being "worker bees" begging God for prayers to be met that you yourself don't believe in. He can't bless something that you don't feel that you deserve. Come on Sarah get with the program and stop doing your own wrong thing. I'm just saying!

To deserve something is often thought of as doing something or having or showing qualities worthy of some type of reward or to be well earned, merited, warranted, justified, fitting, appropriate, and suitable. The good news here is that God adopted you into His family in spite of who you are, your history, your looks, and when He allowed Jesus, His only son, to die on an old rugged cross so that you can be all that you can be in enjoying all of the goodness of life it is up to you to feel like you deserve this privilege and walk in the blessings of knowing who you are! Ginna in Virginia walked around all day long feeling that she deserved whatever blessings she was relaxing in and enjoying the other lady walking around methodically always serious, up tight, overweight, diabetic, more week at the end of her check than money, no vacation, car broke down, mad, frustrated, overwhelmed and intense because she was accepting of simply being there and doing whatever she was told to do. One person's normal was happy and carefree the other person's normal was up tight, over worked and under paid.

Whatever you set your mind to doing and your imagination to feeling you can achieve it if you simply have faith and believe in what your inheritance is as the Father cannot see you He only feels what energy you emit along with the sweet smelling aroma of that feeling. It is not hard! In fact, it is so easy that people make it hard, because they don't believe how easy life really is supposed to be. I once heard Curtis J. Jackson III say to Oprah during an interview that people were going to have to pray or worry, but not do both! Good feelings purely mean that you are happy, rested, excited, passionate, and wholeheartedly enjoying the life that you have been gifted to live!

This brings to mind a poem I discovered when I was in the 10th grade at Northern High School in

Flint, MI that I read for a Public Speaking class that was written by Max Ehrmann called Desiderata:

> Go placidly amid the noise and haste,
>
> and remember what peace there may be
>
> in silence.
>
> As far as possible without surrender
>
> be on good terms with all persons.
>
> Speak your truth quietly and clearly;
>
> and listen to others,
>
> even the dull and the ignorant;
>
> they too have their story.
>
> Avoid loud and aggressive persons,
>
> they are vexations to the spirit.
>
> If you compare yourself with others,
>
> you may become vain and bitter;
>
> for always there will be greater and lesser persons than yourself.
>
> Enjoy your achievements as well as your plans.
>
> Keep interested in your own career, however humble;
>
> it is a real possession in the changing fortunes of time.
>
> Exercise caution in your business affairs;

for the world is full of trickery.

But let this not blind you to what virtue there is;

many persons strive for high ideals;

and everywhere life is full of heroism.

Be yourself.

Especially, do not feign affection.

Neither be cynical about love;

for in the face of all aridity and disenchantment

it is as perennial as the grass.

Take kindly the counsel of the years,

gracefully surrendering the things of youth.

Nurture strength of spirit to shield you in sud-

den misfortune.

But do not distress yourself with dark imaginings.

Many fears are born of fatigue and loneliness.

Beyond a wholesome discipline,

be gentle with yourself.

You are a child of the universe,

no less than the trees and the stars;

you have a right to be here.

And whether or not it is clear to you,

no doubt the universe is unfolding as it should.

Therefore be at peace with God,

whatever you conceive Him to be,

and whatever your labors and aspirations,

in the noisy confusion of life keep peace with your soul.

With all its sham, drudgery, and broken dreams, it is still a beautiful world.

Be cheerful.

Strive to be happy.

Upon completion of reading the poem and looking up the students were watching me in complete silence I thought it was a flop until suddenly they exploded with claps and one student with tears rolling down her face said that was so beautiful and I thought silently to myself "wow"! You are probably thinking what does this poem have to do with this declaration that You Deserve well it has everything to do with you knowing who you are and Whose you are by accepting your God given gifts, abilities, and talents and not imitating someone else's gifts, abilities, and talents.

Open your arms to receive the good feelings that are to be embraced by you. Strengthen that feeling so you feel as good as you can as often as possible and if not always at least starting off at about 51% of the time. You have a right to be here just like the trees and the stars. Get into the habit of feeling passionate about good emotions when you think about anything that is important to you such as your health, family, career, love, money, success and prosperity think with the understanding that you deserve the best! Recognize that life is responding to your feelings as we are magnetic beings and you do attract good or bad to you knowingly or unknowingly. The law of attraction is fully operational and in effect regardless of you wanting it to be or not. You don't see gravity, but you know if you step off of a 10 story building without a device to help you float or fly you will fall and there are no "if's", "ands", or "buts" about it! The choice is yours right now and going forward to know who you are and Whose you are with the remarkable knowledge that the Father will respond to you according to your feelings. Remember, everything in life inclusive of every decision you make are all based on your feelings about any given situation or circumstance so take the time to feel good. You Deserve it!

If you don't know then let me tell you that God is the type of Father that will tell you something you should know in order to make your life better, but He is not going to force anything upon you as He believes in free will and meeting you at your faith is what He will do just as He told the two blind men in Matthew 9:27 – 29 (KJV). And just like all caring parents he left his last will and testament (the Bible) so that you can read it for yourself to make sure you are accessing all of its blessings designed to make your life better not harder. You cannot do this by listening to what someone else is telling you with that old Sarah spirit meaning well, but wrong as all outdoors! When they have read and understood the last will and testament left by our Father and still proceed to re-arranged the scriptures to mean what they want it to mean, because they're thinking that God cannot or maybe will not do what He says He'll do and as a result people will be enslaved for years all because of a know it all spirit twisted the rules to meet their justification instead of the Creators intentions and indications. The Father has said He is no respecter of persons and will meet you at your level of faith so believe that you receive what thus says God and not Sarah and save yourself and your generations grief and heartaches. Do you have faith enough to believe that You Deserve to have all of the goodness of life? Then all you have to do is know who you are and Whose you are! Once again this isn't hard unless you make it hard by the choices you make, because really and truly You Deserve the best in life!

Here is a little example of a young lady's ideology about "deserving" for herself and her community. A few years ago I was channel surfing looking for wholesome entertainment on the television and I saw a local news reporter interviewing a young lady about 12 years of age along with a group of excited youth and a few of smiling adults. Wanting to know the reason behind the happy faces I put the remote down and began watching the news program. The excitement was the result of a local young lady that had been born and raised in the area that had become an Olympic Gold Medal Champion and she was returning home! The excitement was in the air and hometown folk had gathered at the Olympian's training center to welcome her home! It was exciting to watch seeing the smiling faces of all the youth as they scurried around talking about their hometown hero. I think I may have glimpsed a couple of youngsters shadowboxing in the background as the interview was taking place. The reporter asked the young lady her thoughts about the Olympian's recent accomplishment and innocently the girl told the reporter that not much good happens to people from her city so celebrating this Olympic athlete was a big deal to her and that maybe someday she could be an Olympic athlete or possibly do something else. As she said "do something else" the excitement in the young lady's voice kinda trailed off as her expression shifted from excitement to doubt. Watching this interview I was happy for the Olympian and for the 12 year old girl but my thoughts lingered on the "something else" pondering what the "something else" could be in the mind of this young lady as she was so very happy and excited for the Olympian and wished her well in her endeavors, but she sounded skeptical about whether she herself could unquestionably be or do something as wonderful like the Olympian had.

This goes back to the earlier concept of praying for the success of someone else, but not so much for yourself or being happy for the success of someone else, but not truly believing that you yourself can accomplish wonderful things in your own life. I'm sure the 12 year old doesn't realize how excited she sounded for the athlete, but the excitement dwindle as she talked about herself doing something great. The feelings of self-worth and being, having, or doing something amazing didn't shoot forth from the 12 year old as she spoke in terms of herself, but she was over excited when talking about the success of someone else. I believe that the good that a person desires for another must be desired for yourself as well. Perhaps she was embarrassed to speak about herself achieving such accolades and felt more comfortable talking about the success of someone else which is more common than not! Like that 12 year old young lady I too for years had thought others were worthy of success and having their dreams and desires manifest, but never saw myself as successful beyond a certain point. This is probably one of the many reasons that Marianne Williamson, the American author, lecturer and activist, told us that playing small does not serve the world. There is nothing enlightened about shrinking so that other people won't feel insecure around you. We are all meant to shine as baby's do when they are young enough to not care about what other's think of them. When they cry everyone jumps

to see what's going on and to figure out how to pac-
ify them. We're checking diapers, getting bottles ready
to feed them, holding them, rocking them, singing to
them doing everything possible to not let them cry or
feel uncomfortable in any way. Baby's are smart too!
They learn that they don't even have to do a full cry all
they have to do is fret pretending that they are going to
cry and the frenzy of activity start as they smile enjoying all of the attention. And as we let our own lights
shine, we unconsciously give other people permission
to do the same. As we are liberated form our own fear,
our presence automatically liberates others. I pray that
beautiful young lady discovers that God will meet her
at her level of faith and will give her the desires of her
heart regarding whatever her heart's desires may be!
Because it is God that gives the desires of the heart in
the first place! He is not going to place something in
your heart and then not provide the way of materializ-
ing the desires after all His Word says "Beloved I wish
above all things that thou mayest prosper and be in
health even as thy soul prosper and I will give thee the
desires of your heart (3 John 2 and Psalm 37:4 (KJV)!
Feelings of unworthiness does not serve anyone in

their life's accomplishments and comparing one's self to others will certainly cause skepticism in the hearts and minds of the individual compelling him/her to underachieve and perhaps not live up to their full potential of their own greatness! So take a deep breath, open your eyes, stand tall, be brave in your own heart and mind so that you too can do great things maximizing your own God given gifts. Young lady where ever you are whoever you are You Deserve"!

We all deserve to experience the best that life has to offer us and believe it or not according to what our minds believe we can achieve! We are worthy of absolutely fabulous life experiences! Certainly, we should be happy for others and we should always desire the best for them, because the Holy Scriptures teaches us in Galatians 6:7(KJV) to be not deceived; God is not mocked: for whatsoever a man soweth, that shall he also reap! Therefore, whatever thought seeds we sow in the garden of our own minds we will manifest that harvest in our lives be it unbelief, lies, truth, bliss, love, prosperity, health or happiness we are magnets and we will manifest in our lives whatever it is that we constantly think about, dream about and talk about. Now keep in mind that when a seed is planted it doesn't grow to it's full potential the next day! Remember it takes time to grow in the dark, warm, dampness before coming to the beautiful light. The seed of a man is planted in the dark, warm, dampness of the womb of a woman where it is fertilized and allowed to develop and grow over a time period of 9 months before the fully developed baby crosses the threshold of incubating inside of someone else's body to being strong enough to enjoy all of the benefits of having its own body. So don't be doubtful when you find yourself in the growth environment of dark, warm, dampness take this time to learn, because the light is coming!

This brings me to another God given opportunity I was given to experience and learn from. I had the privilege of being in a public school setting of a 5th grade English class and the discussion was on careers and college education at local colleges and universities. Every 5th grade girl in the class that volunteered her opinion to the dialogue of goals and desires for themselves as they grew into adulthood each one of them wanted to do hair in their kitchen (not go to cosmetology school), have three kids and get an EBT card (a state issue cash benefits card). When they were asked about becoming something like a nurse or an accountant they each replied "no, that is too hard". What they did not understand is regardless of if they study to be a hairstylist, astronaut, nurse or firefighter they will still have to study their craft in order to become an expert in their chosen field in order to receive the necessary credentials to prove that they are qualified to do what they're doing to earn a living. An EBT card, doing hair in the kitchen and three kids were all they could see in their futures. Once they were told that they would have to attend and graduate from cosmetology/barber school to pass a state test in order to get license to do hair regardless of if she is working from home or in a salon one girl immediately said "then I don't know" and her young friend looked at her and replied "me either".

Also, in that same 5th grade class about five boys professed that they wanted to be professional basketball players and when they were told that every boy their age in the United States of America and abroad wanted to be a professional basketball player! They all looked kind of discouraged, perplexed, and overwhelmed at the thought of that many boys wanting to play in the NBA. One of the boys said "then, I'm not sure what I want to do" looking defeated before he even got started then he asked "are you sure every boy my age wants to play in the NBA?" The reply was this is not to discourage you from wanting to play in the NBA but to encourage you that you have to put in the required work of being the best basketball player that you can possibly be and to get the best grades that you can possible get so that you can play for your current school, then continue with keeping your grades up so you can play for a college or university with hopes of being drafted by a NBA team! Please listen, because as he thinketh in his heart, so is he...Proverbs 23:27 (KJV)! I hope the following Biblical principle Numbers 13:30-33 (KJV) makes sense to you in relating it to the 5th grade class and that is: And Caleb stilled the people before Moses, and said, Let us go up at once, and possess it; for we are well able to overcome it. 1 But the men that went up with him said, We be not able to go up against the people; for they are stronger than we. And they brought up an evil report of the land which they had searched unto the children of Israel, saying, The land, through which we have gone to search it, is a land that eateth up the inhabitants thereof; and all the people that we saw in it are men of a great stature. And there we saw the giants, the sons of Anak, which come of the giants: and we were in our own sight as grasshoppers, and so we were in their sight.

The reason they were told how many other boys their age dream of becoming National Basketball Association players was to get them to think of preparing to be the best by putting in effort, time, energy to a goal that they wanted to accomplish not to burst their bubble causing them to not want to even try to be the best that they could be. In trying to motivate them to greatness the opposite happened, because of the way the class saw themselves of NOT being deserving of accomplishing their goals! Once they heard of the competition it was easier for them to let their dreams go out the window than try to come up with a plan to be the best student athlete possible in order to one day do what they desired to do, play basketball. Please believe You Deserve!

2

Health is sometimes accepted as "it is what it is since it runs in the family" and the family could be bloodline family, church family, cultural family, and race family! For example I've heard people say they are susceptible to certain dis-eases, because they are African American or that prostate cancer runs in their family, but I beg to differ because health along with everything else is what we develop it to be in our thought process from deep down in the recesses of our minds of years of giving energy to a dis-ease. Job said "what he feared has come upon him; what he dreaded has happened to him" chapter 3 verse 25 (KJV) . People take on the health beliefs of the people they are around be it their race, their gender, the commercials watched on television, their tribe, their parent(s) and/or generations of known illnesses in their family tree otherwise known as generational curses. We all deserve excellent health since it is our birthright to be in health and we should be educated that our Creator says Beloved, I wish above all things that thou mayest prosper and be in health, even as thy soul prospereth 3 John 2:2 (KJV). But if you take a look around there are sooo many unhealthy and struggling to survive people. The difficulties of some people to perform simple day to day functions of activities of daily living of simply being alive is truly too staggering to conceive! What I've discovered is it is expensive to be sick! Only rich people can afford to be sick but most of them are off enjoying life! So whose left to "buy in" to the get sick is inevitable mindset is the working poor and the poor! Is this an oxymoron since the working poor and the poor can't afford to be sick, but are the segment of society that are sick! Again, I repeat: Beloved, I wish above all things that thou mayest prosper and **be in health**, even as thy soul prospereth 3 John 2:2 (KJV)! What about this scripture is misunderstood? The Creator of all things desires for us to be in health. Baby, You Deserve to be healthy!

I know it is easier said than believed, because once upon a time I was one of the poor sick people! I didn't like it mentally, physically or financially! I decided that excellent health is a combination of mental and physical health working in cooperation, collaboration and conjunction with my feelings and thought life creating my well-being or the lack of my well-being. I decided that my health is just that my health that I have been gifted and it is up to me to do with my health what I see fit. I can choose to be or not to be sick! I could nurture my health and within the abilities of my mind along with exercise, nutritious foods, clean water, fresh air, deep breathing and understanding my thoughts, feelings, and emotions I can activate my birthright of being in the best health possible from birthday to birthday, because God has said Beloved, I wish above all things that thou mayest prosper and be in health, even as thy soul prospereth 3 John 2:2 (KJV)! I began exercising. I began eating more nutritiously high quality food. I began controlling my thought process of how I saw my body. I pictured me in the recesses of my mind being happy and healthy all of the time! I acknowledged my body operating and functioning in the perfection which God created it to operate and function from the crown of my head to the soles of my feet and all parts and spaces in between all the way down to my molecular level. Within a matter of months my arthritis was gone! My breast issues were gone! My anemia was gone! My weight was normal! My blood pressure was normal! You see I resisted the enemies of arthritis, breast issues, anemia, obesity, abnormal blood pressure and they had to flee from me! After all as a child of the most high God I'm (we're) directed to submit (y)ourselves therefore to God. Resist the devil, and he will flee from you (KJV)! Excited about my progress I wanted all of my family to experience what I had experienced with going through a metamorphosis in my overall well-being. I changed my thoughts, emotions, conversation, activity and ultimately my life and I began sharing what I had done and what I was doing to overcome my health issues with people I loved and more often than not with people that I'd never seen before and will probably never see again. Excitement was having a field day in my emotions of the goodness of God!

I have family members living in a city that was experiencing a "rough spot" as I've heard it called due to the act of simply quenching ones thirst with a tall cold glass of water or bathing in a warm bath of water was causing skin outbreaks on many people young and old, lead poisoning in some, and many other mental and physical dis-eases that was affecting thousands of people in a real populated city right here in the good 'ol U.S. of A. and one comedian had the audacity to jokingly tell one of the residence of the city on a live radio show to enjoy his tall glass of brown water... Really!!!

Once upon a time this community was a prospering community that had major corporations thriving in the community and everyone was healthy and happy. But these corporations that were providing financial means to the city had long left the community and financial opportunities of being gainfully employed unfortunately left with the major corporations. Public schools had closed and the city's population had dwindled down to a mere population of about 80,000 give or take and a lot of that 80,000 were out of work. I once heard a lady being interviewed by a local news station say that the people that remained in the city were sickly poor people and that they could not afford to leave the city or otherwise they would be like the other people that have already left – they'd be gone! Immediately my mind thought of my family that are still there and I thought about when I was sick I was paying a co-payment every time I went to visit the doctor and to every specialist I was being sent to and the only thing that was getting better were their finances as I continued to give them my money each time I was seen in their offices! I was buying medication and feeling worst and worst! This was a vicious cycle that I became determined to break! The money I had used on medicine and doctor visit co-pays I could have been using towards getting my family out of that city, going on vacation, buying an education that will grant me the opportunity to become gainfully employed in some other avenue either in the city or out of the city.

I told my family they had to make a decision that health, well-being, and a life free of medication was what they wanted as they would let their food be their medicine and their medicine be their food which was a suggestion given to the world by Hippocrates, an ancient Greek physician. I advised my family and friends to continue taking whatever medication that their doctors had prescribed to them, but to start eating foods consisting more of fruits, vegetables, grains, bottled water, juicing some of their meals, fish, ashwagandha, spirulina, and a list of other ingredients that could help in the restoration of their health to a homeostasis level of well-being.

Seriously, I advised them to look forward to excellent health and to begin to visualize healthy, whole, complete functioning bodies and they had to own those feelings and believe those feelings taking charge of their health and well-being. My advice was for them to look at pictures of themselves of times gone by when they were enjoying excellent health and strength and they were in a happy frame of mind. Suddenly, I began following my own advice on a more structured level and changing my mind's thought process in order to change my life even more so than what I already had and little by little like a germinating seed I began to recover and blossom in my health! Because I totally believe that good health begins in the recesses of the mind and that every cell, fiber, atom of the body down to the molecular level knows what you are thinking and feeling and will manifest those thoughts and things into reality in your body and shows up on the screen and stage of your life! You Deserve!

I believed that if I got my thoughts right and lined up with 3 John 2:1 Beloved, I wish above all things that thou mayest prosper and be in health, even as thy soul prospereth (KJV) that I could be back to my fantastic self in no time and the good news is you can, too! Just like the scripture called you "Beloved" allow me an opportunity to use that term of endearment as I say please believe me "Beloved" this scripture is for us all! If you are reading this book then this scripture is for you! If you are sick in any degree be it as simple as allergies or major as colon cancer do an inventory of yourself to find out what is in the recesses of your mind! What you think about ultimately you will bring about in the demonstration of your life, because Proverbs 23:7 (KJV) for as he thinketh in his heart, so is he and please keep in mind that You Deserve excellent health and well-being by the renewing of your mind! That is: I beseech you therefore, brethren, by the mercies of God, that ye present your bodies a living sacrifice, holy, acceptable unto God, which is your reasonable service. And be not conformed to this world: but be ye transformed by the renewing of your mind, that ye may prove what is that good, and acceptable, and perfect, will of God - Romans 12:1-2 (KJV).

Now let me be clear in saying that I've not gone to medical school not one day in my life! Nevertheless; I've lived quite a few years on this planet and I've observed quite a few sick people in my life time. I have worked in a teaching hospital on the East Coast and a medical clinic for surgeons that was affiliated with that same East Coast teaching hospital, I have a Bachelor of Science in Psychology degree and my specialty is in Industrial Organization Psychology and I've read numerous metaphysical causes of illnesses, studied Biological Psychology, Addiction Theories, Massage Therapy modalities, Respiratory Therapy, Arterial Blood Gasses, The Holy Bible and as a result of my training I have decided upon the following list of dis-eases that may be manifesting in your bodies without you realizing the thought processes behind the dis-ease. I implore you to look over the list of dis-eases and the subconscious thought process that sometimes accompany the dis-eases and mental disorders. What I recommend is to take a look at the list of dis-eases and the emotion that generally accompanies the issue and be truthful with yourself in how and/or if this is something that you are experiencing. Start a journal write down how you feel and why you feel the way that you feel and once you have worked through your emotions and you have all of the information written in the journal have a "Cremation of Cares" ceremony and burn the journals and go free to be the best you that you can be!

Abdominal Cramps = Fear

Abscesses = Agitating thoughts over past hurts

Accidents = Inability to speak up, Rebellion, Violence

Aches = Longing for love or to be held

Acne = Disliking one's own self

Addictions = Running away from self

Aids = Feelings of hopelessness, Sexual guilt

Alcoholism = Inadequacy or Self-rejection

Allergies = Irritated about current life

Alzheimer's = Inability to face life as it is

Anemia = unwilling to use talents in service to others

Anxiety = Distrust of the natural flow of life

Arteriosclerosis = Hardened narrow-mindedness

Arthritis = Anger, Resentment, Stuck, Limited

Asthma = Unresolved guilt, Suppressed crying

Back Aches = No support of life

Bad Breath = Anger and Revengeful thoughts

Baldness = Fear and Tension

Belching = Fear

Bladder = Anxiety

Bleeding = Anger

Blood Issues = Lack of joy

Blood Pressure - High = Longstanding unresolved emotional issues

Blood Pressure – Low = Lack of love as a child

Body Odor = Fear, Disliking one's self

Bowels = Can't let go of the old

Brain = Stubbornness

Breasts = Putting others first, Difficulty in giving love

Cancer = Deep hurt, Secret grief

Cataracts = Dark future

Cholesterol = Clogged joy channels

Cold Sores = Fear of expressing anger

Depression = Anger, Hopelessness

Diabetes = Longing for what might have been

Diarrhea = Running away from something/ someone

Elbow = Inflexibility, Rigidity

Eye Sty = Angry at someone

Feet = Not wanting to move forward

Female Problems = Self Denial

Flu = Responding to mass negativity

Headache = Self-criticism

Heart Attack = Money issues or poor position over the joys of life

Impotence = Sexual guilt and/or pressure

Indigestion = Anxiety about a recent or upcoming event

Kidneys = Criticism, Failure, Shame, Undissolved anger

Knees = Stubborn, Pride

Liver = Fear, Anger, Hatred

Lungs = Grief, Unworthy

Menopause = Fear of no longer being wanted

Menstrual Imbalance = Guilt

Overweight = Fear, Over sensitivity, Denied love

Pneumonia = Desperate, Tired of life

PMS = Giving away power

Psoriasis = Fear of being hurt

Prostate = Guilt, Inadequacy

Rheumatism = Feeling victimized, Lack of love

Sciatica = Hypocritical, Fear of money and the future

Seizures = Running away from self, family, and life

Sinus = Irritation to someone

Sprains = Anger and Resistance

Sterility = Fear

Stomach = Fear of the new

Stroke = Insecurity, Lack of self-expression

Swelling = Painful ideas, Stuck in thinking

Thyroid = Humiliation

Tumors = Attending to old hurts

Ulcers = Not good enough

Varicose Veins = Over worked, Over burdened

Vertigo = Scattered thinking

Wisdom Teeth = No mental space for firm foundation

Now, keep in mind that the above lists are my observances only as I've come across people of all walks of life throughout my observation/research as a Spiritual Being on this earth's journey. I am advising everyone to please seek medical advice for any and all illnesses that you may be experiencing and follow your physician's advice and pharmacological recommendations and perhaps if you are stable enough to work in conjunction with a metaphysician, personal trainer and dietician that can advise you on the best foods to eat for your body's overall health and well-being to try to completely heal your whole entire body from the inside out by all means do so, because You Deserve the best life has to offer you!

Knowing the above list of dis-eases with corresponding mental anguishes I decided to read all I could on various ailments and on my next appointment to see my Primary Care Physician I mentioned my thoughts about my list and she told me it was a matter of me "taking my power back owning my feelings and taking responsibility for my health" in conjunction with using medication until the medication is no longer needed. I thought "what, take back my power!" Well, I left her office lost in thought of when did I give my power away and to whom did I give it to? The one thing for certain was that whoever had my power were costing me major money due to the health issues I was experiencing which made me determined to get my power back! Now, the rest of what she said was sitting on the back burner of my mind while I figured out how to get my power back.

After reviewing my list for the 5th time while sitting quietly peering out of my back patio door the realization came to me as the light bulb clicked on in my head that the one constant emotion and/or feeling behind each dis-ease is fear. Fear is the driving force of causing so much anguish and discomfort in so many people's lives and they are not even aware that fear is their number one culprit! I became certain that most people were like me and not recognizing that fear had a quiet grip on their existence placing their lives in a complete choke hold. My mission had been handed down to me by the God I serve and I was prepared to let everyone know what I had discovered as I agreed to assist them in discovering their freedom from this quiet culprit. One of my assignments became apparent to me which is to let everyone know if you rid your-selves of this culprit, the spirit of fear, and allow the light to shine on the darkness which can be thought of as **F**alse **E**vidence **A**ppearing **R**eal and see the situation for what it truly is that you would and could rid your-selves of the dis-eases that is afflicting your lives. For

God hath not given us the spirit of fear; but of power, and of love, and of a sound mind 2 Timothy 1:7 (KJV) and Job said for the thing which I greatly feared is come upon me, and that which I was afraid of is come unto me (KJV). What are you afraid of? It is time for you to face the conscious and unconscious fears.

Keep in mind, that previously I mentioned that if you healed your mind then your body would be made whole and by changing your thought process you would change your life! I did a re-interpretation of this and understood this to being an attempt to change your circumstances before changing your mind or your thoughts would be a fruitless attempt in changing your circumstances. You have got to change your mind first! As this was my vicious cycle of taking medication to cure something I had not gone within the recesses of my mind to resolve within me first! Without changing the thought processes of my mind I was in a never ending cycle of symptoms, agitation, visiting the physician, purchasing prescriptions, referred to specialist, considering surgery, re-fills on the prescriptions, changing the prescriptions to see if something else would work better, and with all of this I was spending my money for this vicious cycle instead of circulating my money to enjoy life! As you probably know when you spend your money it never returns, but when you circulate your money it always comes back to you. Therefore, my questions are: What are you thinking about? What are you talking about with yourself and with others (private conversations)? What is continuously on your mind consciously or subconsciously? I ask you to monitor your thoughts like a micromanager with nothing else to do, but watch what you are thinking!

Now this can be interpreted even further to being if you don't heal your mind then the rest of you can forget about ever being healthy and that is un-deserving which is majorly opposite of what we are talking about which is being in a position of living without known and unknown fear and living with power, love, and a sound mind, because You Deserve an improved enriched life!

Friends, because I "feel" the need for a prayer right here and right now agree with me if you will that every chain, bondage, spell, and any form of witchcraft directed towards you and your family are broken.

Every evil, negative word, act, or deed that has risen up against you and your family in judgment is condemned as this is the heritage of the servants of the Lord, and your righteousness is of God. You and your family are encapsulated in the love of God with fires of protection and hedges of protection all about you and around you and no thing (nothing) shall harm you and thanks be unto God as He receives all of the glory in Jesus name right here and right now on this day we decree and declare it as being so!

Trust me when I tell you that prayer changes things!!!

· · · · · · · · · ·

3

* * * * * * * * * *

Stress can be silent but deadly! The difference between good health and bad health is an extraordinary life of fulfillment, joy, health, wealth, love, accomplishments, travel, leisure and premature death due to sickness, depression, risky behavior, ill nutrition, and various dis-eases. One of the leading causes of bad health is bad stress! Stress is a way that the body responds to activities of daily living that are both positive and negative. Good stress and bad stress. Stress is like Dr. Jekyll and Mr. Hyde by keeping us alert and productive, fight or flight, and on the other hand it can rear its ugly head and tear us apart and be like the evil spirit in Acts 19:15 and the evil spirit answered and said, Jesus I know, and Paul I know; but who are ye (KJV)? Stress is so fierce that when it gets finished with you your family will be calling for the undertaker and fighting over who gets what if a last will and testament was not left behind instructing everyone on what to expect and what not to expect. Well this book is here to help you overcome the stressors of life by planting the seed thoughts of the deserving life that you should be experiencing! Think about this why would the Creator of all things have His only begotten son to die on a cross for sins that he didn't commit for people that would go through hell on earth! What kind of love is that? 1 John 4:8 (KJV) He that loveth not knoweth not God; for God is love and for love shall cover a multitude of sins 1 Peter 4:8 (KJV). I know you have heard the story about the old Cherokee that told his grandson, "my son, there is a battle between two wolves inside of us all. One is evil: it is anger, jealousy, greed, resentment, inferiority, lies, and ego. The other is good: it is joy, peace, love, hope, humility, kindness, empathy, and truth". The boy thought about it, and asked, "Grandfather, which wolf wins?" The old man quietly replied, "The one you feed".

So I ask you; which wolf are you feeding? Bad stress is that evil wolf that is the wrongdoer behind so many dis-eases and will sneak upon you before you know it and within a twinkling of an eye you have suffered a stroke, a heart attack, or some other unexpected physical and/or mental ailment like a nervous breakdown! When the wrong feelings of un-necessary fatigue, stomachaches, muscle pains, headaches, indigestion, anxiety, sadness, restlessness, mood swings, over eating, under eating, drug abuse, alcohol abuse, cancer, and social withdrawal to name a few wrongdoing symptoms sneaks in like a thief in the night watch out! Because stress has you by the family jewels and will squeeze all of the life out of you! Remember John 10:10 (KJV) the thief cometh not, but for to steal, and to kill, and to destroy: I am come that they might have life, and that they might have it more abundantly. Don't you want an abundant life? After all You Deserve to enjoy the plushness of an abundant life is your birthright!

Since knowing is half the battle and even though at the time of me writing this book I'm not Rhodes Scholar I am going to help you get on your way to living a stress free life! The Source of all things, God, is no respecter of persons and what He did for me He'll do for you, too! To them who by patient continuance in well doing seek for glory and honour and immortality, eternal life: But unto them that are contentious, and do not obey the truth, but obey unrighteousness, indignation and wrath, tribulation and anguish, upon every soul of man that doeth evil, of the Jew first, and also of the Gentile; But glory, honour, and peace, to every man that worketh good, to the Jew first, and also to the Gentile: **For there is no respect of persons with**

God. For as many as have sinned without law shall also perish without law: and as many as have sinned in the law shall be judged by the law; For not the hearers of the law are just before God, but **the doers of the law shall be justified** Romans 2:7-13(KJV).

My sincerest suggestion to you is for you to face all the deep dark fears that have been holding you captive for too many years of your life and take your power back! Yes, I discovered who had taken my power and it was all of the past issues that had caused major stress in my life that I had never resolved. I taught myself how to live with the stressors until the affects of the stressors began to kill me softly with dis-eases in my mind, spirit, and body. When my family physician said to me with a stern look on her face "take back your life" it shook me to my core! I thought when did I give my life away? I began soul searching. I began facing fears. I began accepting things I'd made excuses for in the past. I admitted to hurts and unresolved anger. With each issue that surfaced in my mind thus therefore my life I reintroduced myself to it and I truthfully allowed my feelings to surface sometime with tears streaming down my face and sometimes with hot anger, fist shaking, and feet stomping. It didn't matter the emotions that surfaced, because what I needed was to allow the emotions to surface so that they could properly be dealt with and put to rest once and for all sent to the sea of forgetfulness Micah 7:19 (KJV).

Ephesians 4:22-32 (KJV) That ye put off concerning the former conversation the old man, which is corrupt according to the deceitful lusts;

And be renewed in the spirit of your mind; And that ye put on the new man, which after God is created in righteousness and true holiness. Wherefore putting away lying, speak every man truth with his neighbour: for we are members one of another. Be ye angry, and sin not: let not the sun go down upon your wrath: Neither give place to the devil. Let him that stole steal no more: but rather let him labour, working with his hands the thing which is good, that he may have to give to him that needeth. Let no corrupt communication proceed out of your mouth, but that which is good to the use of edifying, that it may minister grace unto the hearers. And grieve not the holy Spirit of God, whereby ye are sealed unto the day of redemption. Let all bitterness, and wrath, and anger, and clamour, and evil speaking, be put away from you, with all malice: And be ye kind one to another, tenderhearted, forgiving one another, even as God for Christ's sake hath forgiven you.

Please understand that fear of all kind when indulged in your mind to excess gets woven into your muscle memory, the crevices of your mind, the flow of your blood, the marrow of your bones and causes negative stress to release negative chemicals into your body temple which causes dis-eases in your body temple and anguish in your mind, because what you think about continuously by replaying scenes of some form of negative circumstance or situation in the movie theater of your mind will only work itself out in the symptoms and dis-eases of your body. What you think about ultimately your bring about! 1 Corinthians 6:15-20 (KJV) Know ye not that your bodies are the members of Christ? shall I then take the members of Christ, and make them the members of an harlot? God forbid. What? know ye not that he which is joined to an harlot is one body? for two, saith he, shall be one flesh. But he that is joined unto the Lord is one spirit. Flee fornication (stress). Every sin that a man doeth is without the body; but he that committeth fornication sinneth against his own body. What? know ye not that **your body is the temple of the Holy Ghost which is in you,** which ye have of God, and **ye are not your own?** For ye are bought with a price: therefore **glorify God in your body, and in your spirit, which are God's.**

Acknowledge the stress! Face the stress! Write the stressors down if you are unable to speak about the stressors at that moment in space and time and even be like one particular group that meet in California every year and have a Cremation of Cares ceremony or call it the Cremation of the Stressors ceremony it's your cremation for your situations so you can call it whatever you like just as long as the point of the matter is to release those issues that are causing you the unnecessary stress (fornication) in your body which is causing you all type of negative health issue. You have an earache ~ why? Arthritis is in your knees ~ why? Wisdom teeth giving you pain ~ why? Check the list and see what your ailments and stressors your body is telling you to deal with. Micro-manage your emotions and body or your emotions and body will micro-manage you!

Practically, every dis-ease listed above has fear listed as a culprit, but when you know Whose you are you can do the seemingly impossible by being brave enough to confront the seemingly impossible and turn that battle cat into a kitty cat by demanding that False Evidence Appearing Real get out of your temple at once! Get like your Intercessor, Jesus! Matthew 21:12-13 (KJV) says Jesus went into the temple of God, and cast out all them that sold and bought in the temple, and overthrew the tables of the moneychangers, and the seats of them that sold doves, and said unto them, it is written, My house shall be called the house of prayer; but ye have made it a den of thieves. Oh yeah, it is doable and Thomas Dexter Jakes, Sr. says "it'll work if you work it" and remember God has not given us the spirit of fear; but of power and of love, and of a sound mind 2 Timothy 1:7 (KJV) and ye have not received the spirit of bondage again to fear; but ye have received the Spirit of adoption, whereby we cry, Abba, Father Romans 8:15 (KJV), therefore; again I say You Deserve to be to blessed and not stressed!

Now that you know what is behind the health issues and you have dealt with the culprit of stress and you have faced the little kitty cat that initially you thought was a raging battle cat and now the tides have begun to turn in your favor. You are turning things around so be diligent in the dark, warm, damp environment of incubation knowing that when you make it to the light you will be well able to stand your ground of who you are and Whose you are! While we have come a long way we still have a ways left to travel. You are on this path of doing good, thinking good and feeling good now let's get your body nourished and hydrated by eating plenty of good foods consisting of nuts, fruits, vegetables, drinking water, and of course exercising after all You Deserve to look good and feel good!

Calm down, I'm not telling you to only eat nuts, fruits, vegetables, drink water, and exercise see you are stressing out for nothing! Break the habit and stop stressing! I'm telling you to have the majority of your food ingestion be of nuts, fruits, vegetables, and water. Consult a nutritionist, because I've not gone to school for that either just like I've not gone to medical school to become a medical doctor I'm working on becoming a Doctor of Philosophy which is acquiring a doctoral degree not medical doctor I want to help you with the root of the problem and get that situation resolved. I don't want to medicate your symptoms and keep you forever coming back in a vicious cycle. I want you to move on, baby, upward and forward! Back to the food conversation at hand; I know what works for me and you have to discover what foods will work best for you and believe it or not if you are eating everything and anything there is a chance that gluttony maybe an issue for you! Tell the truth and shame the devil! Let me be the first to tell you that you shouldn't eat everything, but discover what works best for your body and keep in mind You Deserve to experience the best health possible and you can't do that with that gluttony spirit in you ~ cast gluttony out of the temple of what should be the temple of the Holy Ghost!

Now that you have calmed your nerves from initially thinking all you could eat were nuts, fruits, vegetables, drink water and exercise! Well, I'm already out on a limb so yes you will have to exercise on a regular basis a minimum of 4 times a week and I know the norm is 3 times a week, but we are not norm type people we are excellent in Christ, Jesus, so we go above and beyond the normal worldly expectations and we do the God thing in terms of what His expectations are for us as our Father!

Therefore, exercise, exercise! Get it in ~ get it in!!! For all of you that have to know the "why" behind things here is the "why": exercise releases endorphins! Endorphins interact with the receptors of your brain that **reduces the perception of pain** and **triggers a positive feeling in the body** that is comparable to morphine which is where the phrase of a "runners high" comes from. For those of you who are now thinking I've gone just a little bit too far well I understand your judgment but keep reading. We are going to get through this I promise you even though I do have some stuff that is coming up that may cause you to have to get your eyelashes glued back on so stay strapped in as we continue down the rabbit whole of ridding our lives of the silent killer called stress!

For those of you that is imperturbable with the concept of moving your body and working up a healthy sweat pat your selves on the back because you are good to go and the repetitiveness of me saying You Deserve is sinking into your subconscious mind and the acknowledgment that you are deserving of the best just because you exist thoughts are yours to be celebrated! But don't get it twisted my Mr. and my Ms. The requirement of you doing your part is still high priority! You have to be a willing participant actively seeking improvement without becoming complacent because you already know so keep applying these principles to your life by micro-managing your mind into the concept that You Deserve to be healthy and stress free! Period! Point blank!!!

When you exercise your body releases natural peptides that will activate your opiate receptors that will cause an analgesic effect to kick in and you know this concept, because so much of this concept is talked about as it pertains to the "runners high" and I advise you to take the advice of Psychologist, Ralph Smart, and breathe in that good Prana, baby! Get yourself out in nature and inhale! Yeah, we getting high off of the natural effects of having a body in motion so that it can staying in motion from birthday to birthday. We are higher than Georgia pines off of the natural endorphins created by the Creator of all things! All you have to do is exercise your way to that euphoric feeling and excellent health and recognize the "runners high" as natural as going to sleep at night and awakening in the morning. So please don't choke off of this natural chemical, because if you do you have no clue of what this book is here to do! This book is created to set the captives free, baby baebey! If the Son therefore shall make you free, ye shall be free indeed John 8:36 (KJV)!

I know and understand that just the thought of exercising for some people causes stress to rise in their bodies when the very thing we are trying to eliminate is stress. So keep it simple! So for starters try 20 minutes a day of nonstop movement of having fun by getting up and moving your body however you feel. Do what you like! Do it how you like! You can move to the beat of a drum or orchestra it really doesn't matter just move nonstop for 20 minutes! Next do 15 minutes of basic weight lifting by using your own body weight or by using the weight of your baby as you lift little Ukie Bukie in the air 20 times the baby will be having a great time, because you are spending quality time with her. She don't have to know you are exercising in fact she'll care less that you are exercising, because she is just enjoying being the focus of your attention. You can use weights you have purchased from a retailer or recycle 1 liter water bottles by filling them with tap water, screwing the top on tightly, and lifting them into curls or triceps pulses be imaginative what body part you work on is up to you in the privacy of your own home, garage, or backyard and don't forget to drink plain water with no additives such as powders and liquids that people so often pour into their water to alter the taste. Just drink plain water as your thirst quencher (if you must add something to the water in order to drink it then add a lemon or lime wedge to your otherwise plain water). Just keep it simple, because the simpler it is the easier it is to stay on the routine of creating a better you!

Now, the best kept secret with all of this is that you will begin to look and feel GORGEOUS in no time at all from the inside out and as you know what's on the inside inevitably manifest to the outside! On the other hand, of course you have professional options such as joining a gym, employing a personal trainer, and joining exercise groups that train for particular causes. There is so much out there so go explore to see all that you may like and get active in as many ways as possible. If you are not ready for that type of a commitment perhaps you will be better off adopting an adorable four legged friend to be responsible for by allowing it to walk you, cherish you, and love you. But whatever you do don't train your four legged BFF to go outside stay within the perimeter of the backyard and come back in when it's ready to return to the comforts of the house.

By walking, dancing, lifting weights, and simply moving will keep those endorphins flowing and if you adopt a four legged friend you become responsible for someone/thing other than yourself and you get to teach the new best friend how to sit, play catch, and walking on a leash instead of the four legged friend really energetic walking you by pulling you by the leash in the direction he decides to go. Whatever method you choose to get fit is your personal preference what is important is that you take your personal health and well-being into reason and you are proactive to health instead of reactive to dis-eases. So get active! Get moving! Buy bikes for you and a family member and ride on the bike trails at your local park. Go skating. Buy a mini trampoline or rebounder and jump, jump, jump to it! Join a yoga class (my favorite is hot yoga), a tennis club, a hiker's club just get moving after all You Deserve to look your very best and be medicine free as the new stress free you!

An amazing secret of exercise is that it uses up oxygen in your system and this causes your body to be responsive to loosing oxygen and burn up stored fat which helps you to control your weight and perhaps even cellulite. When I lived in Virginia I had the privilege of going to one of the many military bases there to visit a fitness center. My personal trainer had calipers for measuring my body mass and body fat and all types of charts and advice, but the one thing I remember most is that he told me even if I didn't do any of the exercises that he showed me that if I would simply walk at least 4 miles a day four times a week that I would burn about 1,600 calories which would be about a half a pound a week. At the time a half a pound a week sounded so futile to me that I shrugged it off as he continued to explain in 6 months without changing my eating habits I'd lose 12 pounds and in a year I'd lose 24 pounds. It was so simple it was too simple for me to comprehend the effectiveness of this method at the time, but a few years older and a lot of years wiser I now appreciate his wisdom.

At the time I wanted a quick fix I didn't want to wait a full year to drop 24 pounds. I wanted the weight gone the day before yesterday even though it took more than one day for the excess weight to get on my body. I could not see the forest through the trees after all at that time I had a microwave mentality of now, now, now! I want it now!!! My attitude was "hey I am going to the event next week and I need to fit into the dress next week so how can we make the weight leave me now for next week not 6 months and 24 months! Rome wasn't built in a day; you didn't gain the weight in a day, and you are not going to release the weight in a day!

Also, now I know I can exercise in short bursts throughout the day called mini workouts. I started walking the halls of my work during my lunch period and doing wall pushups behind my desk, lifting my computer to stand while I typed, using an exercise ball to bounce while I watched my favorite 30 minute television show, and parking at the end of the parking lot when going into buildings. By figuring out how to move my body to do mini workouts I began to notice a lower heart rate, better mood, my complexion improved, my weight began to decrease and I began to feel better from the inside out! Because my muscles were starting to change for the better! They were becoming elongated, defined, stronger and I was looking good! I've always known that muscles burn more calories than fat, but because I was naturally muscular when I was younger (I get it from my paternal grandmother) I never concerned myself with maintaining my muscles. Oh but now, at 50 + I am maintaining my muscles on a regular basis since my muscles will burn calories even when I am not working out please believe me knowing is half the battle and doing is the other half!

Unfortunately, for most women our bodies will tend to lean toward fat so working out daily to stay strong and in shape is a must if you want to look good all the way to your 120th birthday! Don't laugh it is possible. And the Lord said, My spirit shall not always strive with man, for that he also is flesh: yet his days shall be an hundred and twenty years Genesis 6:3 (KJV) and you thought I was making that up…um huh. Don't you know if my days shall be 120 years then I want to be in good health and in my right mind operating as my own caretaker! The scripture doesn't say 120 years laying in a sick bed with someone feeding you, bathing you, and partially having empathy for you. I know a God that so loved the world, that he gave his only begotten Son, that whosoever believeth in him should not perish, but have everlasting life John 3:16 (KJV) didn't intend for our 120 years in the earth realm to be sick and feeble who would want that for their children? Certainly, not a loving Father! Do you want your child to be sick, feeble, and depending on someone else to do all of their activities of daily living for them? Of course you don't!

In 2017 I had the privileged of meeting a 97 year old man that lived in my apartment complex in Las Vegas, Nevada. He was an Pacific Islander and he swam every day for exercise and boasted about feeling as well as men two times his junior. He said his only medicine was the food he ate, the love he carried in his heart, and the water he drank. His encouragement to us all was to do the same: eat good food, practice love, exercise and drink water.

I want you to think about Matthew 7:11(KJV) which says if ye then, being evil, know how to give good gifts unto your children, how much more shall your Father which is in heaven give good things to them that ask him? Why would God give us (his children) the opportunity to live to be 120 years old and then cause us to be old and feeble trying to make it to 120 years? What a cruel, stressful, contradiction and unusual punishment that would be!

Exercise is a stress alleviator and a mood enhancer! Remember the runner's high we talked about earlier? When I was experiencing the worst bout of stress in my life my health care workers all kept telling me the same thing: Exercise! They all encouraged me to exercise more than to take the medicine I was being prescribed! I knew that exercise would reduce stress hormones in my body which would get my blood pressure down to allow the good endorphins to activate and improve my mood, but I was caught in a mind trap! Phillipians 4:8 gave instructions by saying brothers and sisters, whatever is true, whatever is noble, whatever is right, whatever is pure, whatever is lovely, whatever is admirable—if anything is excellent or praiseworthy—think about such things. I, on the other hand, was thinking about everything except those things! My mind was on who done me wrong, when they did me wrong, why they did me wrong, what I could have done, what I should have done, and if I ever get a chance to see them again what I was going to do, what I was going to say and how I was going to say it! Then Isaiah 26:3-4 (KJV) became alive in my spirit that God would keep me in perfect peace if my mind is stayed on Him... trust ye in the Lord forever: for in the Lord Jehovah is everlasting strength!!! Not to mention the fact that it was imperative that I get my blood pressure down, because low and behold it had shot up to 187/111! Like David I had to ask the question of who were these uncircumcised Philistines, attempting to defy the child of the living God - 1 Samuel 17:26 (KJV)? David had 5 smooth stones and a slingshot I had and have the promises of God according to Romans 12:19 Dearly beloved, avenge not yourselves but rather give place unto wrath: for it is written, Vengeance is mine; I will repay, saith the Lord (KJV). Please know I don't wish bad on anyone and those are not my words, but God's Words! Then Exodus 14:14 (KJV) comforted me with the Lord shall fight for you, and ye shall hold your peace and my inner peace came with Him telling me via the Psalms 46:10 (KJV) to be still, and know that I am God: I will be exalted among the heathen, I will be exalted in the earth. Baby, my blood pressure came down and I've been walking in the comforts of who I am along with knowing Whose I am ever since!!!!

I took the advice of the physicians that were attending to my mental and physical well-being at that time and I began to take long walks in the park to relax my blood vessels and breathe in that good Prana to lower my heart rate. I moved to a new state that had beautiful state parks and mountains and I began walked everyday as I oohed and ahhed at the majestic wonders of the red mountainous rocks that were snowcapped and surely my mood elevated, the depression left, I forgot about those uncircumcised Philistines and I mentally began to feel better. Enjoying my clear and free mind I stepped out of my past and into the nowness of life and trust me when I tell you this option is yours for the taking! The promises of God are for us all act like you know Whose you are and before long you'll not have to act you'll actually know. Actual and factual, baby!!! Please believe me You Deserve!!!

Also, if your mind has been in a mental trap house for a long period of time keep in mind you didn't get like that overnight you had lots of practice so it will not be an overnight success of climbing your way out of the mental trap house. Your neurotransmitters that send specific messages from one brain cell to another brain cell that are generally associated with a happy feeling are broken and need to be repaired in order to get the neurotransmitters to stop misfiring. So my request is that you not only exercise your body, but that you exercise your brain, too. Begin picturing the electrical impulses in your brain snapping and firing and attaching back to the necessary cells the electrical impulses that are needed to cause you to revive from a limp and lazy state of being. CPR your mind! Read for the sake of rescuing your mind from the mental trap house it has been in. Read stuff that you previously had no interest in so that you are learning. If your mind wanders which it will do remind it that you own and manages it that it does not own and manage you! Earlier I mentioned you having the ability to live to be 120 years old in your right mind and in good health well determined in your mind to get your 120 years that the scriptures promises us! Be in your right mind while being in your best body/health ever! It's doable or as the one Bishop always say "it'll work if you work it"!

I didn't want to take a pill for the rest of my life to get my neurotransmitters to fire properly so I went on a mission to be my own caretaker so that I could live my life healthy, happy, successful, prosperous, managing money as directed by the Manager of it all, loving and being loved! I am happy you have joined in on this mission to do better and to be better as we press toward the mark for the prize of the high calling of God in Christ Jesus Philippians 3:14 (KJV) living stress free, healthy, well balanced lives! You Deserve!!!

4

Forgiveness, oh snap! Yes we are going there and since we have established that your mental health contributes to your physical health and well-being let us face the battle cat on your pathway of FORGIVENESS! Yes, I'm talking about the "F" word! Don't stop reading now you have come to far to turn back and for God to leave you! Stay focused (whew, another F word)! FOR-GIVE-NESS!!! Matthew 6:15 (KJV) But if ye forgive not men their trespasses, neither will your Father forgive your trespasses. Now do you understand how imperative it is that you forgive? If you don't forgive you'll not be forgiven and who are those uncircumcised Philistines to keep you from your deservable forgiveness?!

Forgiving is going to help you get healed and help some of your blessings that have been held up to finally fall out of the windows of heaven to flow like milk and honey all of you and your family! Remember this is not just about you it's about generational blessings. I know you have heard of generational cursings well get ready to enjoy generational blessings! Hallelujah and praise God! To activate the blessings you have to release all of the unnecessary garbage that you have been carrying around and it has been decaying your body causing all sorts of ailments to manifest from the missing and or graying hairs from your head to the wrinkles on your face that is aging you 40 years like a recent age app that people were playing with on FaceBook! People pre-mature aging, cancer, ulcers and all sort of out of control cells wreaking mayhem in your bodies have to be arrested and evicted and the Word of God is the Sheriff that is going to get them out of your temple! Be like Jesus he was our example to follow and he demonstrated how to put unwanted foes out! I command you to NOT let them uncircumcised Philistines turn God's temple into a trap house! Matthew 21:12 (KJV) tells of us Jesus went into the temple of God, and cast out all them that sold and bought in the temple, and overthrew the tables of the money changers, and the seats of them that sold doves, and said unto them, It is written, My house shall be called the house of prayer; but ye have made it a den of thieves. Do you not know that dis-eases, unforgiveness, stress, worry, hate, and any feeling and/or emotion that tries to strong arm your temple is a thief. You better tell the truth and shame the devil and take back your mind which is ultimately your life! God gave you your life! How and why are you giving your good gift away? Matthew 7:11(KJV) If ye then, being evil, know how to give good gifts unto your children, how much more shall your Father which is in heaven give good things to those who ask him! You are probably saying "I didn't ask God to be born well Suga Baby you didn't ask Him not to be born either and besides you don't remember what you did or said before you showed up on the scene of earth. You could have been begging God to come down here so since you are here act like you are supposed to be here. In other words act like you know! You Deserve!!!

When he went through the temple kung fu kicking, knocking people out of their seats, and turning over tables he wasn't playing! So don't you play with these crazy, earthly, Egyptian dis-eases running amok in your precious body. Exodus 15:26 (KJV) said, If thou wilt diligently hearken to the voice of the Lord thy God, and wilt do that which is right in his sight, and wilt give ear to his commandments, and keep all his statutes, I will put none of these diseases upon thee, which I have brought upon the Egyptians: for I am the Lord that healeth thee. Are you kidding me that you don't know what type of God you serve?! You serve a strategic, warring God! Again I say act like you know!!! So FORGIVE! You can't go wrong with forgiveness! Whatever happened in your past let it go stop running re-runs of the event over and over in the movie theater of your mind. Evict that old stuff and move on it probably happened so many years ago that you have forgotten most of the real details, anyway! Let it go by blessing the situation with love and release those old hurts and frustrations to the God who is the Creator of all things and resides on the inside of you. First John 4:4 (KJV) Ye are of God, little children, and have overcome them: because greater is he that is in you, than he that is in the world, but if you continue to re-play that hurt, pain, and drudgery over and over in your mind you only hurt yourself both mentally and physically again and again. Don't do that to yourself! Stop bumping into the same corner of the table that you know is since no one has bothered to relocate the table from the last time you bumped into it. Walk intentionally around it! What is the definition of an insane person? Glad you asked. It is someone that continues to do the exact same thing over and over again expecting different results! What?!!!

A couple of summers ago I lived in Michigan and one of my cousins would frequently visit me and park at the parking space in the rear of my apartment building and would walk across the grass through the beautiful pine trees in my back yard in order to get to my patio. Once she had made the trek across the grass and she would stop fussing about the trek across the grass we would sit and laugh and talk about the good times we had in our youth and of the newness of consciousness. I really did enjoy those conversations with my cousin who has a very bright mind with quirky sayings that only she says. However, from the parking space that she always parked in and about 15 feet from the front of her automobile once she would step onto the grass and start to walk towards my patio there was a hole of some sort that was in the ground and concealed by the grass around it and not seeing the hole she would step into that hole, hurt her ankle and stumbled out of the hole and complain about the hole for the next 30 minutes as she sat rubbing her ankle. This was an occurrence with each visit! Two weeks would go by and she would call to say she was on her way to visit me now I know the hole is there and she knows the hole is there, but she would mechanically park in the same parking space and fall into the same hole and once again she would complain about the hole the first 30 minutes of visiting with me! She would always say something should be done about the hole before someone falls and breaks their necks. She suggested that I do something about the hole or have the complex managers place a sign there warning people of the hole if filling the whole in wasn't an option, because she was going to consult a lawyer to sue them for lawn and hole neglect. What, are you kidding me lawn and hole neglect! Finally, frustrated with her committing the same actions over and over again in spite of knowing that the hole is there I informed her that every time she visits me she parks in the same parking space and walk towards my patio in the same direct line to my building knowing full well that the hole is there. It's been there all summer it is a hole! It is not going to move and obviously it hasn't been filled in and it will not be filled in. Park in a different space and walk in a different line. I told her I've seen the lawn guys out there looking for the hole, but to no avail. I told her the kids are out there carelessly running around having a good time and no one is able to find that hole to fall into but her. She looked at me and said to my disbelief that I never take her side on anything. You see she was determined to make the fact that she falls into the same incessant hole every time she visits me be someone else's fault. She was refusing to take responsibility for her same continuous actions of knowing possible harm could happen to her if she did the same thing over and over. To put it bluntly this is being stuck on stupid for a lack of a better phrase and being tired of the same foolish behavior instead of opting to be proactive about the hole and walk a different route. A month had passed and the end of the summer was quickly approaching us and finally she phoned asking what I was doing and that she wanted to stop by to enjoy the fresh summer breeze since the weather had cooled off a bit and we hadn't seen each other in a little while. I told her sure come on by that I'd be glad to see her; which she did. This time she parked her car three spaces away from her usual parking space and walked a different path directly to my patio and completely avoided the proverbial hole in the grass that had caused her so much anguish and almost came between us because according to her I never took her side. It took her a month to find it in her heart to forgive me of my reaction to her and hole, but forgive she did.

I tell you this story, because I don't want you to become a creature of habit. Recognize the issues and straight away resolve the issues. I'm not telling you what I've heard I'm telling you what I know. Take positive action to change for the better do not get upset if someone chooses not to participate in your dysfunction of being a creature of habit instead of a creature of change. Be proactive instead of reactive, because You Deserve the best and stop getting upset with people when they don't agree with your foolishness!

Picture this: a beautiful person that is the picture of health with beautiful strong healthy hair, flawless skin, twinkling eyes, pearly white teeth, not too muscular, not too thin, beautiful clothes, smelling good, but carrying a corpse around on his back like an accessory designer back pack. After carrying the corpse a few days the decomposed smell of the corpse is overpowering the smell of the beautiful person who was the picture of health is now becoming a smelly mess! After a little while the body of the corpse will start to cause putrefying ulcers on the body of the once beautiful person and before long the corpse's contamination has spread throughout the once upon a time beautiful person's body until the beautiful person's body is completely destroyed as the dis-eases from the corpse has all together consumed and taken over the beautiful person's body. With time the beautiful person is unrecognizable due to the illness from the corpse which has caused the one healthy head of hair to be mangled and falling out, teeth once were pearly white are now rotting and falling out, ulcerative body sores of decomposition all because of the dead sin of the weight of carrying around a corpse on his back. Horrid isn't it? This is what un-forgiveness will do to your beautiful healthy body. Un-forgiveness is the dead corpse and it will absolutely destroy your beautiful body in just a matter of time. The stench, the sores, the smell, the decomposition, the boils will eat at you until there is nothing there to eat. Un-forgiveness is like a parasite of necrotizing fasciitis it needs a body to thrive on

or otherwise it is nonexistent! Don't let this be you…
FORGIVE! You Deserve to forgive!

You are probably thinking that I don't know the story behind your un-forgiveness and that I don't know what they did to you or how they did what they did to you or why they did what they did to you and the fact of the matter is I don't want to know what they did to you or how they did what they did to you nor why they did what they did to you, because I don't want that petrifying stuff to get over on my back and inside of my mind, but I'm sure there is someone out there that would love to share in your misery so that you can share in their misery especially since misery loves company.

But I am asking you to help me help you and let all of that vulgar stuff go, because every time you re-play the scene on the movie screen of your mind you are only hurting yourself over and over again! Don't wallow in sorrows!! Take heed to the advice of Matthew 7:6 (KJV) and do not give dogs what is sacred; do not throw your pearls to pigs. If you do, they may trample them under their feet, and turn and tear you to pieces.

Therefore, stop replaying that trash over and over in the theater of your mind and telling the same version of how they did you wrong, because not only are you thinking, and talking about it, but now you have other people talking about it with you and now they are talking about it with others, too, and it never goes away. What a mess! Snap out of it! Right here and right now let it go! The day terror and nightmare whatever it may be is no longer serving you! Release the negativity to go live in the abyss never to return to you again. Serve an eviction notice to the problem, situation, and circumstance and evict it out of your life forever! Let un-forgiveness go and let the power of God do its work by casting all your cares upon him; for he careth for you I Peter 5:7 (KJV). This is a directive that God has given to you and as an obedient child do what you are told to do! Cast your cares upon Him since Behold, he that keepeth Israel neither slumber nor sleep Psalm 121:4 (KJV) let the Father deal with the issue and you go free! You Deserve Forgiveness and You Deserve to forgive!

Now that you have forgiven yourself and everything and everyone of your past it is time to get new experiences in this game called life. So on this part of your journey discover your likes, your passions, your love, your faith, your ability to breathe deep and often as you let go and let God be the co-Creator with you in enjoying your time on this planet. Know this that when you were born the sun was already here, the grass was already here, the oceans were already here, the cars were already here, the flowers were already here all for your enjoyment! These things were created by the Creator by Him putting the ideas into the minds of His people to create for you to enjoy! What a loving Father! Go to a museum, go to an amusement park, go on a cruise, try horseback riding, learn a new language, get better at speaking your current language, dance like no one is watching, ride a bike, knit a sweater, write a book, get married, help raise someone else's kids, paint a house, ride in a hot air balloon, go canoeing, rock climb, travel! Do something! Learn something! This stuff was created for you! There is so much to do, to be, and to see why settle for just the block you grew up on or the same route that you take every day to work. Get out there and enjoy life and forget about all of those old hurts, disillusionments, tragedies, and uncircumcised Philistines they are only making you old before your time and sickly. Discover your own likes and watch your soul along with your body begin to heal as Philippians 3:13 - 14 (KJV) says Brethren, I count not myself to have apprehended: but this one thing I do, forgetting those things which are behind, and reaching forth unto those things which are before, I press toward the mark for the prize of the high calling of God in Christ Jesus. Let go of that garbage pit that is causing you to always wanting to meet up with other people that are in the same boat to get lit and while you are in the mood to forgive ~ forgive the most important person that is currently in your life, yourself! We live and learn. Count your mistake as an experience and keeping pressing towards the mark for the prize of the high calling of God in Christ Jesus – Philippians 3:14 (KJV).

When you forgive yourself release those self-condemning thoughts that has attempted to take up permanent residence in the recesses of your mind by placing them into the abyss and never ever never go back to pick them up again, because casting all your cares upon him; for he careth for you 1 Peter 5:7 (KJV) is a Divine directive from our loving Father! It doesn't matter what you did, what you didn't do, or who you did it to forgive yourself and release those negative feelings and demand that they never return to you as you have acknowledged your mistakes and acknowledge that you will not re-commit that same sinful or out of good character action again. As this is what true re-pentance is when you do something that is sinful in nature or out of what should be your good character and then you never do that same sinful or un-natural uncharacteristically thing again. Get the right things on your mind and straighten up and fly right! When the woman was caught in the act of adultery and was about to be stoned for her sin Jesus said unto her, neither do I condemn thee: go and sin no more John 8:11 (KJV). You see when God forgives you and he doesn't throw that old stuff back up in your face again reminding you of what you did or what you didn't do He loves you too much for that type of behavior! So if the Creator of all things says He doesn't condemn you why are you condemning yourself by continuing to think on those things that cause you bodily harm and to hold un-forgiveness in your heart? Think on this:

Revelation 12:9-11(KJV) And the great dragon was cast out, that old serpent, called the Devil, and Satan, which deceiveth the whole world: he was cast out into the earth, and his angels were cast out with him. And I heard a loud voice saying in heaven, Now is come salvation, and strength, and the kingdom of our God, and the power of his Christ: **for the accuser of our brethren** is cast down, **which accused them before our God day and night**. And **they overcame him by the blood of the Lamb, and by the word of their testimony; and they loved not their lives unto the death**!

You Deserve!

5

Happiness is being emotionally and/or mentally well experiencing positive emotions and being content and joyful feeling like life is good in all aspects of life: family, health, romance, career, education, housing, transportation, love, and wealth. Happiness should now be easy to experience with all of the new knowledge or in some cases reminders of what you already knew to come into your life as you have let go of all of the negative experiences that have been running amok in your life. So with all of the negativity you have removed from your life as you have learned how to walk away from people and situations that have threatened your mental well-being, wreaked havoc on your peace of mind, drained you of your self- respect and energy as you recognize that they no longer serve a positive purpose in your life! You have claimed your happiness and you have let go of anger, regrets, worrying, blame, the past, fear, and you have learned that eliminating those uncircumcised Philistines from your life that lied to you and on you! You've let go of those people that disrespected you and tried to use you or put you down behind your back and to your face as they smiled and hid behind the lie of "I'm just playing". No, they are not playing! Because death and life are in the power of the tongue: and they that love it shall eat the fruit thereof Proverbs 18:21(KJV) and what comes out of the mouth proceeds from the heart, and this defiles a person. For out of the heart come evil thoughts, murder, adultery, sexual immorality, theft, false witness, slander... Matthew 15:18-20 (KJV). You are now free from fear and all of the emotional discomforts fear and un-forgiveness caused you and you are living in your happiness and contentment. You are moving onward, upward, and forward in your happiness. You are a mover and a shaker of all things positive, fresh, and new. You can accomplish all of your heart's desires and you know to delight thyself also in the Lord: and he shall give thee the desires of thine heart Psalm 34:4 (KJV), because your happiness is well deserved!

Your mental and emotional state of well-being is so improved you are feeling good and looking good and you are thinking how you are going to accomplish all of the good things that is going to benefit you and others in your tribe affecting your circle of influence in order to positively affect your world of concerns. Your happiness is a breath of fresh air for you and for all that come in contact with you. Your emotional state is an achieved state of eternal healthiness! Your physical state is exceptionally healthy! You are expressing joy everywhere you go and people are excited to see you come into their environment, because joy has become a contagious part of who you are and everyone wants some of your joy. Your disposition is an embodiment of a refreshing breeze blowing on to the balcony off of the ocean sounding like a beautiful sweet lullaby at twilight soothing your mental well-being. Your physical state is healthy and you are agile and mobile looking good in and out of your clothes! Your smile is brighter, your laugh is louder, you jump higher, you notice the sky is clearer, the sun is brighter and others are able to see the difference in your walk, your talk, your style, and your overall well-being. You feel good and you look good. Life loves you and you love life! You wake up singing lyrics to the old musical called Oklahoma's and you don't even know why you have the hook of the song playing in your head since you've never even seen the movie: "Oh, what a beautiful morning oh, what a Beautiful day I've got a beautiful feeling everything is going my way"! You know what everything is going your way, because You Deserve to have everything going your way so don't question it simply enjoy it!

Listen, you are experiencing happiness at a level that you have never before experienced! Happiness levels and opportunities are coming your way on a regular basis and your immune system is so strong, because it doesn't have to deal with foolishness and mayhem it can concentrate on the job it is supposed to do and that is take care of you! Your immune system is taekwondo kicking off the common cold and flu viruses during cold and flu season that everyone else is contracting, but you! The insomnia that was keeping you up all night has been evicted out of your system and has packed up and moved out of your life! Now you are sleeping and enjoying the benefits of REM sleeping and you are automatically sleeping a full 8 hours every night! Good job, because You Deserve it and as a result your appearance is looking youthful, you look rested, and your elimination process is functioning as it should and your organs are enjoying this new found exhilaration of healthy chemicals flowing through your body temple. Life is now starting to look good on you and happiness is no longer a pursuit it is a way of life for you being enjoyed daily as your activities of daily living has become easy, positive, and stress free. You Deserve!

Now that you are open and receptive to the joys of life the Universe is in full cooperation with you and is magnetizing good experiences to you at unexpected times as well as expected times. You are thinking with clarity and decisiveness ready to move onward, upward, and forward!

Now, you have been so focused on you that you haven't given much thought to anyone else so you are humming along in the produce section of the grocery store and begin thumping melons and listening to sounds that you are not sure what they are supposed to sound like, but it is interesting to you none the less so you go through the motion of melon thumping and listening. Suddenly a person that could be of your dreams, but you haven't been dreaming so you think maybe this is someone from your sister's dreams, your grandmother's dreams, looking like Lord have mercy walking up to you with a beautiful bright magnetic smile and says "I've been watching you pick up a watermelon, thump it, and put it back down for about two minutes and you've not made a selection yet are they all bad or maybe you don't know what you're listening for". You look up an recognize it someone you knew from junior high school. Then he asks the million dollar question "do you remember me?" As floods of thoughts of him in gym class, walking down the hall talking with his friends enter your mind you say "of course I remember you" then your thoughts quickly go to yourself thinking you should have put on makeup and a better looking outfit. "Give me a hug" he says as he extends his arms to you. As you hug him back and the cologne he is wearing mixed with his body chemistry causes you to remember feelings you've not felt in a looonnng time. Stumbling backwards you mumble under your breath "Devil, you a lie!" he ask "what you say?" You awkwardly lie yourself by saying "nothing". Then standing next to the watermelon the two of you begin to catch up on each other's lives until he says "let's meet up somewhere for a bite to eat while I'm in town" and you hear yourself saying "I'm on this juicing kick right now maybe the next time you're in town I'll be eating solid foods and we can meet up then" and then you think to yourself are you crazy! I cannot believe you just said that! Then he tells you that he did see on Facebook that you were juicing your foods and you think to yourself that you didn't even know you were friends on Facebook. Serendipity begins to be your new best friend, but you begin to think this can't be happening, because you end up in Virginia and he's in Virginia! What!!! You are in Massachusetts and he is in Massachusetts! Get real!!! You are in California and he is in California! Are you following me?!!! You are in Dubai and he is in Dubai what the freak in frat is going on! This can't be happening! Then you block him just in case he is a stalker and you stop posting your traveling information on Facebook and he still shows up everywhere you are. Then you ask "God, what is going on?" It's as if you hear God's voice deep inside your heart of hearts replying to your question with and the Lord God said, it is not good that the man should be alone; I will make him an help meet for him and whoso findeth a wife findeth a good thing, and obtaineth favour of the Lord – Genesis 2:18 and Proverbs 18:22 (KJV). Then you test the waters and say to him "by the way I'm celibate" and his response is "okay, then I'll be celibate, too; until we get married"! What!!! Girl please, You Deserve! Stop playing!!! You Deserve!

The God force in you loves your new happiness and emotional state of being and will continue to bring exciting new delightful experiences to you. Relax and enjoy them! You purchase a raffle ticket from your 9 year old neighbor who is selling tickets to support his flag football team and the prize is a brand new still in the box 52" television. You give the little boy the $1 for the ticket and tell him jokingly" make sure I win". Him and his little brother walk off smiling because you have purchased a ticket from them and you place the ticket into the key bowl on your sofa table and forget about it. Two weeks later you receive a phone call from the little boys coach telling you that you won the television in their football teams raffle and please pick it up at your earliest convenience or if you desire he will bring it to your house! You tell him that you don't think it could fit into your small car to which he replied that the team would bring it by so they could get a group photo of you with the winning television. You just purchased a big screen TV for $1.00! Life is good! You Deserve!

Your brother is walking through the mall and recognized your best friend from high school whom you have lost contact with since graduation. Your brother gets the phone number gives it to you then suggest you call and adds "he seems like he is still good people". You call your old friend the two of you agree to meet for lunch one Saturday afternoon and as you are getting dressed for the luncheon you try on a dress that you hadn't had on since last summer and you discover you have somehow miraculously lost those last stubborn ten pounds that you had been struggling with for the past three years and the dress fits perfectly! The Universe wants you to be happy and is enjoying bringing happy experiences into your reality. Give God thanks and go enjoy yourself, because You Deserve to be happy and have a good time!

These may all sound like coincidences, but that is how God allows the Universe to work on your behalf with serendipitous circumstances of hunches prompting you to do something, bringing something or someone into your life or to go somewhere at a particular time. Listen to the voice of God that resides on the inside of you and trust what it is saying as this is your true earth's tour guide. Stop reasoning away your hunches, because reasoning has no place in God given hunches. If you keep yourself in the mindset of God knowing his voice by communicating with Him on a daily basis. Talk to Him first thing in the morning upon rising and the last thing at night before sleeping and get in the habit of taking God at His Words on trust! If you take delight in the Lord, he will give you the desires of your heart Psalm 37:4 (KJV). Even if you didn't know your heart was desiring to have a relationship with a loving man of God! God really do want you to be happy! 2 Corinthians 5:7 (KJV) For we walk by faith, not by sight! May the righteous be glad and rejoice before God; may they be happy and joyful Psalm 68:3 (KJV). Please…you know You Deserve!

Now that you know that serendipitous circumstances are coming to you and you are experiencing expected and unexpected happiness it is time for you to become your happiness biggest cheer leader! You have got to start to expect good things to come to you now and always! Know that the Universe, God, Jehovah, Ancient of Days, Alpha and Omega, or whatever of the many names that the Creator of everything is referred to by you please know and understand that because you were born you should experience happiness automatically! It is a part of your inheritance of being a child of God! Happiness in your life according to your submission to His words and His directive, last will and testament of how you should act, think, speak, and live is yours for the taking. Don't get other people's permission to be happy just decide to be happy and enjoy the benefits of happiness! I'm sure you have heard the phrase 'misery loves company' well do not give those uncircumcised Philistines a chance to dictate to you your happiness. The teachings of I Samuel 15:22 (KJV) But Samuel replied: "Does the Lord delight in burnt offerings and sacrifices as much as in obeying the Lord?" To obey is better than sacrifice, and to heed is better than the fat of rams. So you see doing what he is directing you to do is better than sacrificing. You obeying God's words and trusting what He is telling you to do as well as what He has done, is doing, and is going to do, because He change not! Malachi 3:6 (KJV) For I am the Lord, I change not; therefore ye sons of Jacob are not consumed.

Think about it, would you prefer for your child to follow your instructions that you have given him or prefer that he not eat for 40 days sacrificing food because of disobedience? Shame the devil and tell the truth! I don't care what your child has done you would simply prefer for the child to do what was told to them by you and be finished with it! You would probably tell your child "baby, momma, love you! Don't starve yourself for me just simply do as I tell you to do and because I am your loving parent I will do my part in seeing to it that you have what you need and a little more not because you sacrificed, but because I love you and want to see you happy and this punishment is going to hurt me more than it hurts you". In the meantime the child is smart enough to try to reason out of the punishment by saying "momma I love you, too; so don't punish me, because I don't want you to hurt"! Whew, kids are so smart! "But, Linda; but Linda"! So, if ye then, being evil, know how to give good gifts unto your children, how much more shall your Father which is in heaven give good things to them that ask him? Matthew 7:11(KJV). You Deserve!

You are one with the One! He resides on the inside of you and He will not force His ideologies, instructions, directives, and last will and testament on you, but He will allow you to discover what they are if you allow the teachings of His scriptures to penetrate your heart, mind and soul. And Jesus looking upon them saith, with men it is impossible, but not with God: for with God all things are possible Mark 10:27 (KJV) and Jesus said unto him, If thou canst believe, all things are possible to him that believeth Mark 9:23. Happiness is absolute when you know that your inheritance decrees for you to be happy and fulfilled with long life and you don't have to sacrifice for it. Happiness belongs to you just because you are you! You Deserve!

Think of all the possibilities of happiness that are waiting for you to experience it and if you are unsure of the happiness you are to think on in order to manifest happiness in your life here are a few ideas for you: Finally, brethren, whatsoever things are true, whatsoever things are honest, whatsoever things are just, whatsoever things are pure, whatsoever things are lovely, whatsoever things are of good report; if there be any virtue, and if there be any praise, think on these things Philippians 4:8 (KJV). God leaves no stone uncovered in this thing called life. His last will and testament has been given to us to learn from, survive triumphantly, and be happy! He wants us to win the victors cup! He wants us to get the gold medal! He wants us to automatically choose Him and His ways, but He will never force Himself or His ways upon us. He is a loving Father that like any earthly, loving, father wants his children to be happy!

Since you have become your happiness number one fan and biggest cheer leader and you now know that happiness comes from within your own mind's thoughts, emotional feelings, and your heart's desires as God prompts these things from within you! This is a great time to shout for joy! Jump for joy! You only get what you think you deserve so make sure you are mentally giving yourself only the best thoughts ever to think about. Know that you deserve the best and all of those old bottled up thoughts of not being good enough or of all the wrong you have done have been cast into the abyss and they'll never return unless you go get them. Now, if He says for I will be merciful to their unrighteousness, and their sins and their iniquities will I remember no more Hewbrews 8:12 (KJV) why do you keep bringing up what you did to Him?! If He has moved on then find it in your good sense to move on, too! Get excited about the ideology of the possibility of being God induced happy! Relax and be amazed at how serendipitous happiness continue to bless your life as you continuously give thanks to the happiness Giver and Maker of possibilities as you co-create with the Creator of all things wonderful for your life ~ it's your birthright to be happy!

Remember you walked away from everything and everybody that no longer had a positive impact on your life and was causing negative emotions to take up residence in your being otherwise known as un-happiness, un-forgiveness, and dis-eases. You detached yourself from those things and those people that were no longer being a positive part of your life experience especially when their existence was completely negative and opposite of yours. You have now allowed the old raggedy relationships to become totally non-existent which was best for all that were involved. The more you can let go of people and things the fewer obstacles and road blocks are on your path in this game called life and this eliminates a constant struggle making your path narrower, smooth, and leading to the street called Straight. At the same time be grateful for your past experiences, because they taught you how to survive and depend on God. Be grateful for all of the new joy and beauty the Universe is allowing you to experience that is changing your entire outlook on life. You Deserve!

You are responsible for your own happiness and can only point others in the direction they should go, but always keep in mind you can lead a horse to water, but you can't make him drink! Their happiness is not your responsibility, but your happiness is your responsibility. Stop waiting for Mr. or Ms. Right (or in some people's cases Wright) to make you happy and look within your own self and make yourself happy even if you have to stand in the privacy of your bathroom mirror and talk yourself into being happy...do it! Groom yourself: shower, put on your best face, comb your hair, splash on your favorite smell good, and put your best outfit on and command that you will experience happy experiences for the remainder of the day that nothing but good will come to you all day long!

Repeat this with conviction until you believe it or at least fake like you believe it. Look at yourself directly in your own eyes and say out loud so you can hear yourself when you speak "nothing but good comes to me all day long and I deserve to have the goodness of God bless my life this day and every day, because I am one with the One! In Jesus name, Amen"! Now go out and enjoy the happy surprises that God has in store for you, because You Deserve!

Remember I mentioned that I was poor and sick I was at one of my doctor's appointments and another poor sick soul began talking to me and I decided to wish him happiness for the rest of his day. He looked at me and said "lady happiness for me has been few, far, and in between" as he went on to tell of the hard luck life he had experienced until fortunately the nurses assistnat called his name to take him back to be weigh area and to the next private room to wait for the doctor to come in to see him. I thought thank you God for rescuing me from that sad story that would have possibly dampened my mood of happiness. Then I asked God to bring a serendipitous event into his life so that he, too, could enjoy a little happiness.

That is the other thing with happiness you have to protect it like it is pure gold, because in fact it is pure gold! People will tell you their issues and problems, because they are hooked on habitually being sad and blue. If you listen to their sad stories before you know it their hard luck life stories will have you singing the blues with them. Get your happiness meter strong in the lord and in the power of his might Ephesians 6:10 (KJV). Know who you are and whose you are and be determined to be happy, joyful, and content as God allows the Universe to bring happy experiences to you. When people bring up something sad you counter it with something happy and if you do this each time they talk to you eventually you'll notice that Negative Nancy will stop talking to and avoid you like you have the plague. I used to run into those uncircumcised Philistines all the time until God gave the Universe permission to only bring people with a happy continence and happy spirit into my environment and when we get together speaking life and not death when the conversation is over I walk away feeling like sunshine! If you have a history of being negative and you are reading this book and you are now noticing you haven't talked to me in a loonngg while now you know why. I am selective of who I allow into my circle of happiness well-being! You Deserve!

I had transitioned from a southern hospitality state to a Midwestern community and I started a new job that I had wanted and asked God for as I went into the position wanting to experience joy and pleasantness with a little bit of a challenge in learning a new position and a new work culture, but nothing majorly stressful. After all, I would be working with highly intelligent people who were professional and all about making things happen for the better by making a difference in young people's lives in the community. But it turned out my perception of what they should be was just the opposite of the reality of what they were! It turned out that they were a group of people that found delight in hurting other people by belittling them and humiliating them in any way they could including some of the young people that they were supposed to be helping! As the old cliché would have it 'misery loves company' was in full effect and I knew that was not the type of company that I wanted to spend my professional time with. You know you always want to be in the company of people that are smarter and wiser than you are so that you can glean from their knowledge, expertise, and wisdom but what these folks was serving was jealousy, envy, threats it was a mess! These were highly educated and intelligent people and I wondered why they were so miserable and wanted so much to pass that misery over onto others who appeared to be otherwise happy with the lives they were living. Then I realized they were not "authentically" happy and unfortunately it showed in everything that they did and said.

It appeared to me that they were not fond of others who had found happiness is some form or way and that is why there was always negative talk, negative jesting, put downs, lies, compromise, and a lot of other negative activity that I care not to get into any further in order to preserve my happiness on my happiness meter. It was so bad that if a person were to walk with pep in their step they wanted to know why you walked like that and they would dramatically imitate your walk in order to give an exaggerated example of making you look foolish. If you spoke with enthusiasm they wanted to know why you talked like that and try to convince you to use broken English and slang like everyone else instead of speaking with intelligence and enthusiasm. If you took a vacation they wanted to know where you got the money to go on vacation and would suggest that you stole money from the workplace. If you purchased a new car they wanted to know what was wrong with the other car and tell you that you wasted money buying a new car when the car you had still worked. So what are you saying I'm to drive the car until the wheels fall off?! They were instigating people against each other arranging arguments in hopes that the arguments would lead to a fight. It was crazy!!!

This group of people was somewhat different than what I had ever experienced in the work environment in that they were not happy at all and obviously they didn't want anyone else to be "authentically" happy in their lives either. Sometimes the impression or my interpretation of their conversations was that only certain people should be happy and everyone else should be struggling to survive in their little lives. They thrived on negative news and negative activity from each other and from customers alike. Before long I became so disillusioned with my place of work that I dreaded going into the parking lot of that place when having employment should have brought me joy as the duties of the job were not hard. Before long I realized I was being robbed of my peace of mind and my happiness!

I had given away my happiness to this negative environment but once I realized it I became determined to get my happiness back! I sought help to get my happiness mind set back to where God would have it to be and to where it was before I got there happy and eager to live a productive life free from anger, strife, and fear. Since starting this happiness journey I've always wanted to be affective and effective in a positive way for all of the people that God would bring into my experience to enjoy and hope that the people would look pass me to be able to see the God that resides in me.

Finally, the adult anguish and turmoil of being in that atmosphere had its toil on my peace of mind as it all was incredibly unnecessary and the notion came to me that I had spent all the time of spreading as much happiness, joy, positivity as I could and due to the toxic environment the time finally came for me to move on! Being at the crossroad I had a choice to make: I could choose to get like them becoming nasty, mean, with drudgery in my heart or I could choose to leave before that nasty mean spirit took over my well-being. So I got out of there as quickly as I had arrived there and to God be the glory! I tell you this so you can learn from my experience and if you find yourself in that type of environment I encourage you to get out of it quick before that nasty infectious spirit gets on the inside of you and you start accepting that as normal, because it is abnormal! God don't want any of His children to be involved in situations like that. He don't even want His children that are causing the toxic situation to live like that, but He will allow it. Keep in mind He does not push the benefits of His last Will and Testament on anyone and please know that His last Will and Testament will work if you work it!

The thoughts of having never worked at any job in my life for such a short period of time and the feelings of being a failure kept creeping into my mind but then one Sunday afternoon as I was going over my time with that company, my duties with the company and the relationships I had developed (or the lack there of) with the people in the company I realized that sometimes some things and people are placed into our lives for a season, some for a reason, and some for a life time. I must simply learn from whatever time I was given with them for the season that I was in at that time with them and learn from the situations blessing the experiences, and move on with my life and pray that wonderful blessing always come into each of their lives for we all deserve so much better and so much more! Don't live like a savage when you were meant to live like royalty.

I happily surrendered the thoughts of brevity and immediately began looking to the totality of possibilities of what was ahead of me. My advice to each of you is allow people and things to play their roles in your life for whatever time frame they have been placed into your life and when their roles are over appreciate them for whatever they were able to bring into your experience (be it negative or positive), release them, and move forward without glancing in the rearview mirror. Look where you are going not where you have been!

Learn from the experience and move on, because You Deserve the best that this life has to offer!

6

Success. When I was about 7 years old I was watching the movie, Mahogany, and one of Billy D. Williams's lines that I will never forget was "success is nothing without someone you love to share it with"! Even at the age of 7 years old these words has had such an ever-lasting effect on me, and from that day of first hearing those words to this day I remember that movie line and I believe it to be so! I will always remember these words and, I've always unconsciously wanted someone to share in my success be those successes small or great and I've always wanted to share in someone else's success be they small or great.

In middle school (even though back in the day we called it junior high school) there was a cheer that we all said at the boys basketball games: S U C C E S S that's the way we spell Success! Then I was gleaned across the information that success meant different things to different people such as becoming the custodian for a particular company could mean success to one person and becoming the owner of the company could mean success to another person. One person desired to mop the floors of the company and the other person desired to own the company. Nothing is wrong with either person's perception of success. It simply is what it is according to your belief system.

Success is the accomplishment of a goal regardless of who or what the job description or person is. It could be a custodian like I mentioned above and s/he is making sure the property is immaculate and the facilities are running in proper order or the CEO making sure that everyone involved with the organization including potential business partners are more than satisfied with the product and service that is being offered. I've learned if you are not ready to accomplish a particular goal in your mind then you will never receive the rewards of that goal in your life.

Once in the not so distant past I had the privilege of coming into contact with a young woman at a community college that ran a certain department in a teaching hospital and she was a department head at the community college as well. By chance the Universe brought us into each other's lives and began to work behind the scenes for me and unbeknownst to me in creating a position for me working for the hospital in the department that the young woman was responsible for. Denise arranged for me to be hired and had the hospital call me to offer me a position, but she never spoke a word of it to me! As a matter of fact, I was so caught off guard when the woman on the other end of the phone from the hospital's human resources department called me regarding the position. I didn't know the position existed and I had not mentally prepared myself for working and leaving my young son in the care of someone else, because I had just moved to that state. I didn't know a soul to trust with my child and the HR lady told me of a daycare in my area that I could take my son to. Denise had arranged everything! I had a lot to think about and I told them I would have to call them back with a decision, because I was not mentally prepared to walk into this unbelievable blessing! The lady at the other end of the phoned sounded surprised at my request to phone them back and at my reservation on accepting a position that paid real U.S. currency and before hanging up the phone she remarked "Denise must really like you. Okay, if you want to call back you have three days". I agreed to the three days then hung up the phone baffled at what had just happened.

The hospital was 20 miles one way from the apartment where I was living; I didn't have reliable transportation or a babysitter to care for my then three year old son. I sat on the side of my bed and asked God to guide me on what to do next. The flash of thought came to my mind to phone my father in law that lived over 700 miles away from me in a different state to tell him I had been offered a position at a local hospital without my ever applying for the job and that I needed transportation to get back and forth to work.

I had asked my father in law to help me purchase a car before and he had politely turned me down so not knowing what to expect and following God's prompting to call him and ask him again I followed Divine instructions of that hunch to call my father in law. This time was different. This time was Divine timing. Excited my father n law exclaimed "what; they called you telling you when to come to fill out the application and what you needed to start work!" I answered him "yes" as I felt the excitement on the other end of the phone and without hesitation he said "can you fly here and drive back?" I told him I could then he said he would go get his niece who was also my friend and the two of them would go pick out a car for me. He said since we were the same age she would know what I liked and they would get me a car to get me back and forth to my God given job. My son and I flew three hours to pick up an adorable black automobile with fancy gold pinstripes and tan leather interior. It was beautiful and it was mine just for the asking! God knew something I did not know and that is I Deserved to have gainful employment and a new car, but I was still blind to the concept that I Deserve!

God worked out all of the details of the transaction from becoming employed, to getting a new car and including getting a babysitter for my son until my spouse returned home from a 6 month naval deployment. Now God had done exceeding and beyond what I had ever expected, asked, or thought possible. God was successful at opening this door for me and I was successful at walking through the door. For this is he, of whom it is written, Behold, I send my messenger before thy face, which shall prepare thy way before thee says Matthew 11:10 (KJV). God knew what He was doing and He had Denise and my father in law play their parts in this season of my life even though

I didn't know what I was doing in knowing how to grow and develop this position into something that I wanted it to be. I could not see the forest for the trees, because I kept feeling like I didn't deserve what God had given me.

You see this job was what someone else (Denise and God) wanted for me and because at the time I had no idea of what type of job I wanted for me. I didn't know how to make this situation continuously work out successfully for me. At the time I had not successfully formulated in my own mind the type of job I wanted or the type of people I wanted to work with or the type of money I wanted to make. All I wanted at the time was to be in a safe environment in order to raise my son. At the time the job was offered to me I wasn't even sure I wanted to be employed and asked them to let me think about it and call them back! Who does that? What I did was I accepted someone else's desire for me. Generally speaking whatever you are ready for is usually ready for you and if you are unsure than uncertainty is what you'll get in return.

Well as you know I accepted the job, the car, and the babysitter to begin work and I was a quick study. I learned fast and applied all of the principles and techniques I was taught and was told the hospital would pay for my college education in that field of study for my job. The problem I had was I didn't like what I was doing. I had learned to be successful at it, but I did not like it. Not everyone is cut out to work with ill people and some illnesses require not just skills, particular techniques, but the fortitude to stand the smells that accompanies the illnesses. Unfortunately, I could not stand the smells and I was becoming more and more intolerant of the smells with each passing day. I carried coffee grinds in my lab jacket pocket. I rubbed vapor rub in my nostrils, and before long I had almost stopped eating and began to get sick myself. Finally, I could not take what I was enduring in trying to keep my God given job and decided not to take the hospital up on their offer to educate me further in the field, because I would be so sick by the time I would pick up my son that I didn't have any energy to play and teach him things that he needed to know. I gave up that God given job as a result of my inability to tolerate the smells. In spite of the outcome I enjoyed the experience of having God to successfully take care of my every need of this particular job acquisition solely on the basis of me asking God for help, but I still didn't have the full understanding that I Deserved my hearts desires, because God is the one that is placing the desires into my heart!

Now keep in mind that if you are not mentally ready to receive something and you get it anyway it will simply be a matter of time before things begin to happen to talk you out of those negative emotions and situations will begin to happen to remove that person, place, or thing from your existence. What you believe is what you'll receive!

I'm advising you to get ready to receive your success if you haven't already done so in your mind first! Know what you want and how you want it then visualize yourself being successful in it! Prepare mentally for it! Feel yourself having it! Talk and act like it is already yours and take Romans 4:17 (KJV) on trust... even God, who quickeneth the dead, and calleth those things which be not as though they were! Speak, act, think, and feel what you desire into existence so that you get to keep what you desire for the simple reason of You Deserve to have it, because you are a child of God!

Remember we established the concept earlier of success being what you make of it and it differs from person to person. Success for you maybe owning and operating a multi-million dollar business and success for someone else maybe working as a food vendor working from a food cart during lunch time in a busy downtown square. Success is what you make it. Have fun with it. Be creative you will get out of it only what you put into it! The presence and power of the God in you will bring your heart felt success to realization manifesting in a way that will be recognizable to you like an old acquaintance, because the success you are ready for is always ready and waiting for you.

Don't concern yourself with how this process works just know that it does work! For my thoughts are not your thoughts, neither are your ways my ways, saith the Lord. For as the heavens are higher than the earth, so are my ways higher than your ways, and my thoughts than your thoughts teaches Isaiah 55:8-9 (KJV).

Whatever you mentally prepare yourself for, the Universe, the Cosmic Law of the Mind, God, Jehova Nissi, whatever you want to call the One that allows us the opportunity to choose up or down; left or right; good or bad, success or failure ultimately the choice is yours and you can get with Him or you can try to get along without Him which is so much harder to do. Also, if you don't decide for yourself someone else will decide for you what they think success is for you. Why give someone else that type of power over your life. On more than one occasion I gave away my power over what I was doing with my life and what I found was what was good for others was not what was good for me. They were happy for me, but I wasn't happy for myself, because I was pursuing their dreams for me and not my own. Don't become confused on someone else's success and try to adopt your thought process to accept it as your own. Know thyself so that your success is truly your success and your happiness can shine from the inside out as you wear it like love and excitement as you greet each day!

Success is a mindset and you either have it or you don't! Just keep in mind if you don't have what you want you'll have what someone else wants for you. A little girl that live in my apartment complex was a very good tree climber and would climb up the trees and yell down at the other kids that would be nearby outside playing and they would try to climb up the tree but would fall and some would even break branches trying to climb up the tree. The little tree climber would sit in the tree and laugh at the other kid's inability to climb as high as she could. One summer's afternoon the sun was radiantly bright, the sky was crystal clear baby blue, the temperature was a comfortable warm 75 degrees, white butterflies were fluttering carefree across the atmosphere with the back drop of perfect green grass and about three kids were standing at the bottom of one of the many tall mature trees looking up at someone in the tree and talking. The maintenance man for the apartment complex got out of his truck to investigate what the children were looking up at and it was the little girl that I'd seen on many occasions scurry up the tree. I watched as he looked up into the tree with the kids and I saw him talking, point his finger, then put his hands on his hips standing there as if he was waiting for a response. After about 5 minutes he walked over to my patio and told me how he ordered her to come down and she replied "no" and looked away. He demanded that she come down out of the tree right now! Again, she replied "no" and looked away! Thinking because she was a little girl of about six years of age he decided to tell her if she didn't come down out of the tree he was going to go tell her mother and that is what caused her to reluctantly, slowly climbed down out of the tree. Once she got both feet planted safely on the ground he said he told her not to climb the trees anymore or he would be forced to report her to the apartment complex main office and to her mother. He asked did you see her spread her little arms out and I said I saw her. He said as she was spreading out her little arms and looking all around pointing to all of the trees in the area she told him that all of the trees belonged to her and that she could climb them whenever she wanted to. He said she told him all of the trees were hers and that he could not tell her what to do with her trees and he said the look on her face was a face of actually thinking and meaning that those trees were hers to climb. He then said he wasn't going to talk to the apartment complex manager, but because the little girl felt in her heart that the trees belonged to her that he would have to let them know so the manager could let the little girl's mother know to keep her out the trees, because he said if she falls she is going to break her neck! He was both tickled and shocked at the little girl's response and I sat on my patio still watching the kids thinking what a wonderful mindset the little one has and I prayed that she never allowed anyone to take that spirit of freedom from her.

You see in her mind she owned all of the trees and in her mind she was not going to allow someone else to tell her what she could not do with her trees. Needless to say she was reported and her mother was advised to keep her out of the trees for her safety. But in that little six year old girl's mind she owned every tree on the complex and they were all hers to climb freely as she felt the desire to climb, because she could climb them like with speed and ease. That is how you have to know that your Father, God, owns everything! If we are God's children, then heirs of God, and joint-heirs with Christ; if so be that we suffer with him, that we may be also glorified together Romans 8:17 (KJV). Know who you are and Whose you are and as a joint-heir You Deserve to climb all of the trees your eyes can see!

Success is what you make it just like beauty is in the eye of the beholder you determine; you decide what type of success you want to enjoy after all You Deserve!

7

Prosperity. No this is not "name it" and "claim it", but it does have the concept that a prosperous life can be a fulfilling life which we all deserve to have! Every day is not going to be all smiles, because speed bumps will present themselves from time to time so slow down and proceed cautiously learning from the experience. Some years ago I heard a pastor from California say that he had been poor and now he is rich and that rich is much better than poor! I thought when I heard that "no kidding, Sherlock" as I put down the television remote control to see what other bright ideas he would share. He told how the bank repossessed the television in his living room , his car, his children needed shoes, and they didn't have food to eat and now the table had turned and he could buy televisions at will, drove the cars of his desire, his children had more than enough shoes that they could change all day every day, and his new house had a kitchen the size of his original house and they had food and money to spare. He said he went from being needy to helping the needy. He went from being hopeless to being hopeful and his desire was to tell people if he could become prosperous that they too could turn a negative situation around and blossom like a desert rose for Isaiah 35:1(KJV) says the wilderness and the solitary place shall be glad for them; and the desert shall rejoice, and blossom as the rose and Ephesians 3:20 (KJV) says Now unto him that is able to do exceeding abundantly above all that we ask or think, according to the power that worketh in us. Remember what God did for me when I asked for that car? He exceeded my expectations and gave me a good looking operational car! Keep in mind that Jesus looking upon them saith, with men it is impossible, but not with God for with God all things are possible Mark 10:27 (KJV)!

The six year old little girl owned the trees in her mind even though literally she didn't own a single tree on the grounds of the apartment complex, but in her mind there was no way she was going to let some-one tell her what she could do with her trees, because she was going to climb the trees if she wanted to or at least until they told her mother to keep her out of the trees. So you have to get your mind right and be not conformed to this world: but be ye transformed by the renewing of your mind, that ye may prove what is that good, and acceptable, and perfect will of God

Romans 12:2 (KJV). God can better use your talents, your wealth, your health, your love, your existence if it is prosperous than if you are poor down and out begging asking for a handout instead of offering a hand up! How can you give a hand up if you yourself is looking for a hand up? How can you help another if you yourself need help? Matthew 15:14 (KJV) says let them alone: they be blind leaders of the blind. And if the blind lead the blind, both shall fall into the ditch.

For years one of my favorite clichés was 'program your mind and you'll program your life' or 'change your mind and you would change your life'! Yet, I was always in the same boat that others were in and I had no clue of how to follow my own advice that I was constantly giving people and when I would see that person again they would be doing so much better than they had before! I needed to know how to get out of that proverbial boat and get to the other side, because I was fed up with being a double minded woman saying one thing yet experiencing something completely different. I hadn't realized that I was still unbelieving of my rights to deserve and I didn't even know I was mentally sabotaging myself with my own self-defeating attitude.

Then I began to realize I was half of 100 years of age and I needed to do better with my life and I began to seek after God: But seek the first the kingdom, and his righteousness; and all these things shall be added unto you Matthew 6:33 (KJV)!

I wanted to live the prosperous life 24/7 not every now and then and self-sabotaging prosperity in my own mind with my double thinking of saying one thing while believing something else. This was insanity and it was not cutting the mustard with what I would talk about and think about 'sometimes'! I was ready for a new thing, because the same ole same ole had gotten just that, old. Isaiah 43:19 (KJV) says Behold, I will do a new thing; now it shall spring forth; shall ye not know it? I will even make a way in the wilderness, and rivers in the desert! Growing up I had heard the mind is the devil's playground and I realized I had to be intentional and definite with my thoughts all of the time. Not every now and then when something would prompt me by triggering the emotions of wanting to do better and to be better.

I had experienced doing something that someone else wanted for me. I had experienced asking and receiving. So why was it that I was having difficulties achieving a certain level of prosperity and maintaining it and exceed my own expectations? Why was this eluding me? What was I doing wrong? I was perplexed! I was tired! I had had enough! My tired was tired! Then it came to me in the still quietness of my mind that I was not sincere with my thinking and believing, because I was allowing other people's thoughts, the race thoughts, the television, the billboards, co-workers, church members, friends, family and the news just to name a few to program my thoughts and to dictate how I felt. When someone I knew would feel bad, broke, disgusted, and busted they would call me or text me and we'd get together and have a pity party and talk about all who had done us wrong and why only certain people are enjoying life! Sad and blue! Yuk, Yuk, Yuk!!! Well at the time unbeknownst to us that sad and blue was only yielding more sad and blue. We were perpetuating it by giving it so much energy causing it to grown and bigger and bigger. Instead of doing something about it by changing the conversations since our words have power and by changing out thoughts since the thoughts were coming from our hearts and God gives us the desires of our hearts. We needed a change of heart, thoughts and words: But those things which proceed out of the mouth come forth from the heart; and they defile the man Matthew 15:18 (KJV) For as he thinketh in his heart, so is he Proverbs 23:7 Death and life are in the power of the tongue: and they that love it shall eat the fruit thereof Proverbs 18:21(KJV).

What!!! I've been killing my own dreams and desires by the conversations I was having and by the company I was keeping! You know the norm is birds of a feather flock together remember my co-workers that I spoke of in terms of how they all thought the same negativity, because that was the culture of their environment. Well I had stepped into a passive culture of broken dreams and disillusionment with people that always wanted to talk about the wrong that others had done to them and that defeated spirit had got on me and I was determined to get it off of me, because I wanted life and wanted it abundantly! The thief cometh not, but for to steal, and to kill, and to destroy: I am come that they might have life, and that they might have it more abundantly John 10:10 (KJV). I got sooo happy I began thanking God out loud and in my spirit as I yelled out stop the world of this vicious defeated unprosperous spirit I want to get off and I am taking back my life!

Remember the old Cherokee told his grandson, "My son, there is a battle between two wolves inside us all. One is evil. It is anger, jealousy, greed, resentment, inferiority, lies, and ego. The other is good! It is joy, peace, love, hope, humility, kindness, empathy, and truth." The boy thought about it, and asked, "Grandfather, which wolf wins?" The old man quietly replied, "the one you feed." I had been feeding the wrong wolf! Lord have mercy!!! I had been listening to all of the negative news reports, and all of the 'what one can't do' and the 'whys that it shouldn't be done' instead of following the Word of God! I believed in all of the negativity instead of believing in the scriptures of what thus says the Lord! Romans 7:23 – 25 (KJV) But I see another law in my members, warring against the law of my mind, and bringing me into captivity to the law of sin which is in my members. O wretched man that I am! Who shall deliver me from the body of this death? I thank God through Jesus Christ our Lord and Savior! So then with the mind I myself serve the law of God; but with the flesh the law of sin. I said aloud "this nonsense stops right now in Jesus name!!! As a child of the most High God and only true living God I Deserve better and I have made up my mind to do better, to be better, to have better, to look better, to feel better, to think better, to speak better seeking first the kingdom of God and His righteousness!

Seeing the errors of my ways I immediately began to change my mindset in order that I may change my life! I said out loud: "Father God, I see my erroring ways of thinking I am better than others and the fact is that I am the same as others and Your Word in Galatians 6:3 (KJV) tells me that if a man think himself to be something, when he is nothing, he deceiveth himself and I have deceived myself long enough! You have spoken to me about pride on numerous occasions and I've not changed from my wicked prideful ways even though I know Proverbs 16:18 (KJV) says pride goeth before destruction, and a haughty spirit before a fall. Teach me how to rectify my thoughts, my aims, and my ways. For it is not about me, but all about You and I can do nothing without You, because Your Word in John 15:5 (KJV) has taught me that You are the vine, and we are the branches: He that abideth in me, and I in him, the same bringeth forth much fruit: for without me ye can do nothing says God. Teach me thy way, O Lord; I will walk in thy truth: unite my heart to fear thy name Psalm 86:11 (KJV). Lord, I cry unto thee: make haste unto me; give ear unto my voice, when I cry unto thee. Let my prayer be set forth before thee as incense; and the lifting up of my hands as the evening sacrifice. Set a watch, O Lord, before my mouth; keep the door of my lips. Incline not my heart to any evil thing, to practice wicked works with men that work iniquity: and let me not eat of their dainties Psalm 141: 1 – 6 (KJV). Thank You for showing me ~ me and I repent this day as the kingdom of heaven is at hand Matthew 3:2 (KJV) in the mighty name of Jesus, Christ of Nazareth!"

Now this may not be your relationship with the Creator of all things and it doesn't have to be, because this is my relationship with the Creator and this is what I did to begin to humble myself. Your relationship with the Creator may have you to go a complete different direction down a complete different path and that is completely normal for we are all unique in Him. As He guides you and you listen to His voice you will know exactly what He will have you to do in order to prepare yourself for whatever blessings are in store for you. He meets each of us at whatever point of need we are currently at and He says in John 10:1 – 5 (KJV) Verily, verily, I say unto you, He that entereth not by the door into the sheepfold, but climbeth up some other way, the same is a thief and a robber. But he that entereth in by the door is the shepherd of the sheep. To him the porter openeth; and the sheep hear his voice: and he calleth his own sheep by name, and leadeth them out. And when he putteth forth his own sheep, he goeth before them, and the sheep follow him: for they know his voice. And a stranger will they not follow, but will flee from him: for they know not the voice of strangers.

This is telling you if you don't program your life to the broadcasting signals of what the Father is telling you then you are being programmed by the world point of views that are contrary to how and what God would have you to do and to be. God's success is different from the world's success. God will put you in places that people of the world will tell you are impossible to reach and after God's placement is realized by others then they will asked perplexedly how did you get that position or how did you get that house or how did you recover so fast from a dis-ease that most people die from? God is true according to Romans 3:4 (KJV) let God be true, but every man a liar; as it is written, that thou mightiest be justified in thy sayings and mightiest overcome when thou art judged and God is real his ways are not our ways Isaiah 55:8 – 9 (KJV) For my thoughts are not your thoughts, neither are your ways my ways, saith the Lord. For as the heavens are higher than the earth, so are my ways higher than your ways, and my thoughts than your thoughts! Wow… stop playing people and take God at His Word!!!

You want something then give something be not deceived; God is not mocked: for whatsoever a man soweth, that shall he also reap Galatians 6:7 (KJV). I lived in a large farming community for 6 years and I learned their way of reading the seasons and the weather. Fall is the time of year that the earth gives forth a harvest from what was planted four to five month earlier. This is also one of the reasons that the holiday of Thanksgiving is celebrated in the month of

November it gives us an opportunity to thank God for abundantly increasing the harvest of what was planted months ago. The farmer gives seed to the earth and the earth gives a harvest to the farmer ~ sowing and reaping. You want a compliment then give a compliment! You want love then give love (not sex, but none physical love)! You get what you give! This concept is plain and simple! No degree required just basic information of you only get to keep what you give a way which is one of the most memorable things that I learned from Michael B. Beckwith!

The same as a farmer that has planted his seed during seed time he then waits patiently for the harvest and you have got to learn how to give before you can receive. If you have $50.00 and you have a bill that is $500.00 don't eat the $50.00 by buying lunch and flushing it down the ceramic bowl! Instead, give that money as a seed by investing it towards furthering the gospel good news, or purchasing pampers for someone else's baby and be amazed at how God will multiply that $50.00 back to you and you are now a wonderful philanthropist enjoying the opportunity of being blessed so that you can be a blessing!

Remember, if you desire God's abundance then obey what He has instructed you to do! 1 Samuel 15:22 (KJV)...Hath the Lord as great delight in burnt offerings and sacrifices, as in obeying the voice of the Lord? Behold, to obey is better than sacrifice, and to hearken that the fat of rams. You know what that burning desire of your heart is! You know what He has told you to do, but you keep putting it off! Why? You know what thus says the Lord to your soul! Stop thinking about it and be about it!!! Obedience is better than sacrifice and the secret of living is giving! Give of yourself! Give of your time! Give of your laugh! Give of your talents! Give of your smile! Give of your love! Give of your positive thoughts! Give of your joy! Give of your money! Give of your energy! Learn to be a joyful giver! Give, and it shall be given unto you; good measure, pressed down, and shaken together, and running over, shall men give into your bosom. For with the same measure that ye mete withal it shall be measured to you again Luke 6:38 (KJV). Every man according as he purposeth in his heart, so let him give; not grudgingly, or of necessity: for God loveth a cheerful giver 2 Corinthians 9:7 (KJV). You Deserve to be a cheerful giver!

Face it; you will never get something for nothing! If you want a good, positive relationship with someone you will have to give your time and energy to establishing that good, positive relationship. Some years ago, I was attending an Easter Sunday church service and the whole service was all about 'giving until it hurt'! Well, the God that I know loves a cheerful giver not a hurting giver and 2 Corinthians 9:7 (KJV) teaches every man according as he purposeth in his heart, so let him give; not grudgingly, or of necessity: for God loveth a cheerful giver! It doesn't mention a hurting giver and I could not wrap my mind around that concept of giving until hurt concept then and years later the concept of giving until it hurt still escapes my comprehension. I just knew I didn't want to hurt as I gave. So be happy about your giving. Seek God for guidance in all that you do regardless of if you are giving time, a smile, clothes, money, advice, whatever and He will give you Divine Intelligence to figure out according to His promptings of who and/or whom to give and what to give! You are one with the One and he guided you to give towards the purchasing of this book and He will guide you to give the information of this book to someone else for their edification and enjoyment, too. You Deserve!

Personally, my life was in need of everything so I began to cheerfully give away a little bit of everything I had: donating blood, smiles, positive comments, money, time, clothes, shoes, hand bags, jewelry, pots and pans, recipes, food, a ride to the store, furniture. You name it I was giving it away! I began looking around my residence for items that were good enough to give away deciding on what was a treasure to give and what was once a treasure that had seen it's better days. People are always saying one man's trash is another man's treasure ~ please stop playing! Don't give someone your trash! At that time my employer gave out achievement awards in the form of gift cards please I became the gift card queen. I put in a lot of energy to win those gift cards and I would get so excited every time I'd win a gift card and one day a co-worker asked me what I did with all of my gift cards and I said I give them away. "What" she exclaimed "you give them away"? "Yes, and the people I give them to get so excited and I love to see their faces when I give it to them". I became a giver and I loved it! Find organizations, churches and people to give to and enjoy their appreciation. I found that I never had to look far to find someone in need and the more I gave the more I received! The Universe always gave back to me as a result of the love gifts and offerings I was giving.

I programmed myself for good things by doing good things. I gave love and received love. I gave shoes and received shoes. I gave money and I received money. I gave compliments and I received compliments and James 2:17 (KJV) says Even so faith, if it hath not works, is dead, being alone For as the body without the spirit is dead, so faith without works is dead also James 2:26 (KJV). Become self-active and begin to master your environment for our purpose in life is to grow and to develop, but society has programmed us to think we are to grow old, feeble, and die. I believe that to be a lie and the truth is nowhere in that! That's human race thought not God thoughts! Give, and it shall be given unto you, good measure, pressed down, and shaken together, and running over, shall men give into your bosom. For with the same measure that ye mete withal it shall be measured to you again Luke 6:38 (KJV). Take God's Words on trust! Matthew 4:4 (KJV) but he answered and said, it is written, Man shall not live by bread alone, but by every word that proceedeth out of the mouth of God. Following God's Words is not hard it is what you make it and it will work if you work it!

You are not prevented from attaining success by where you were born, who you were born to, or how you were raised. God has given you the opportunity to choose higher thoughts, proper thoughts to get you to a higher mental level so that you can attain the desires of your heart. So, therefore; delight thyself also in the Lord: and He shall give thee the desires of thine heart Psalm 37:4 (KJV). You Deserve!

I was visiting my mother when suddenly I felt the need to stand still it was the strangest thing, because I felt like what is going on. Perplexed, I sat down on her sofa and looked at the contents on her table and a 4 inch green and white cross with an ivy vine inset was sitting in front of me as it had been sitting in the middle of her table for years. I had always noticed it but I had never read it. Casually, I picked it up and the following scripture was on it: Psalm 46:10 (KJV) Be still, and know that I am God! I had begun feeling like a mouse in a cage running on the proverbial hamster exercise wheel going nowhere fast! I wanted off of the spinning wheel and out of the mouse cage! I knew I deserved more than a shoe for a shoe and a hug for a hug. I had started feeling disappointed with everything I was doing and I had stopped realizing the grace that God was bestowing on me. I had stopped appreciating God and I began feeling like is this it? Could this possible all that there is? I felt like there had to be more and if there was more out here than what I was experiencing then why wasn't I experiencing it? I wanted more from my life! Then I heard the lyrics of the lyrical genius, Shawn C. Carter, saying "just let me be great!"

Then I realize that everything I was desirous of resides within me and God lives inside of me so all that I wanted would come from my deepest desire to be more; to do more; to see more; and to not accept the common human race thought of status quo working hard toiling to get enough money to pay my mortgage, pay a car note, pay school loan, buy food, buy shoes, pay my mobile phone bill, and whatever other day to day living expenses that I had. This desire to be more; to do more; to see more was an extension of God who lives in me! 1 John 4:4 (KJV) Ye are of God, little children, and have overcome them: because greater is he that is in you, than he that is in the world!!! These feelings of being more, doing more, seeing more are God's inherent feelings wanting to be expressed through me.

Prior to God sitting me down on my mother's sofa and prompting me to read the little cross that had always been on the table that I was a lighthouse for God and that when people looked at me I wanted them to look pass me to be able to see the God in me. Yet, I had placed God in my little small box of giving. Now, He was telling me to sit still and know Him! I agreed to decrease so that He could increase John 3:30 (KJV) in me demonstrating His desires for His people! I understood this to not be about me, but all about Him. This is God's show not Joan's show! I stepped down off of the "giving thrown" that I had created and said "God, I surrender all I am a willing participant of being the clay allowing you to be the Potter work through me removing out the wrong element from my life and bring in the correct element to my life so that You can be You in my life".

God's prosperity is our prosperity, because we are one with Him for he that is joined unto the Lord is one spirit 1 Corinthians 6:17 (KJV) and me desiring to be more; to do more; to see more is God that resides on the inside of me seeking to express a fuller life through me. No longer would I feel uncomfortable about desiring to be more; to do more; to see more and going forward I would allow God's full expression through me and I realized my life had been stuck because of the negative feelings I possessed about prospering. I didn't feel deserving of prosperity and I secretly shied away from it. I would self-sabotage a situation to prevent myself from prospering "all out". Emotions more often than not is stronger in manifesting what we feel than the double language of what we say: one minute saying something positive about ourselves and then cancelling it out with something negative. I asked God why had I been fooling myself and secretly avoiding prosperity? Sitting in a North Las Vegas public library the following poem by the 13th century Persian poet Rumi came across my computer screen:

"The breezes at dawn have secrets to tell you
Don't go back to sleep!

You must ask for what you really want.

Don't go back to sleep!

People are going back and forth

across the doorsill where the two worlds touch,

The door is round and open

Don't go back to sleep!"

Knowing a little bit about synchronicities I looked up from the computer screen and whispered "okay, God, I'll not go back to sleep". That night I woke up at 3:30 I began counting the hours I needed to sleep to be fully rested and went back to sleep. The next night I awakened again and I remembered I wasn't to go back to sleep and I lay there in my bed looking at the light shining through the blinds of my bedroom window and I have no clue of when I went back to sleep. Upon awakening I apologized to God for falling asleep and I felt the inclination of being advised that the next time I was to get up out of bed and sit on my balcony. I thought God are you sure, because it will be dark outside and someone will be out there. He answered within my spirit reminding me that I lived in a gated community and that He hadn't given me the spirit of fear. So excited about my date with God I went through my day happy with anticipation wandering what God would reveal to me. Again, 3:30 am finally arrived and this time I got out of my bed and went out onto my balcony in the quietness of the moon lit night and the breeze was so pleasing and smell of the Cerdidium Desert Museum tree outside my bedroom window was so amazing that I crossed my legs and opened my arms and said "thank You, God; for waking me up ~ this is wonderful and peaceful!" I enjoyed it so much that I began brewing tea to sip while I was out there enjoying the night breeze. After months of sitting out there enjoying the night breeze a lady walking a little white dog was out there and a black car moving slowly down the street going in the opposite direction. I thought all of this time I've been out here I'd not seen anyone or anything else and tonight there was major action going on! Whew, I put my cup of tea on my little table and sat up in my chair preparing to go inside when I saw one of my relatives sitting across a table in a kitchen say to me when I was a teenage girl that I was never going to amount to anything and that I'd be an alcoholic/drug addict with a house full of kids turn into a lesbian and be poor for the rest of my life! I felt the salty tears run down my face and I sanked back into my chair and the joy left my body as I recalled the pain of those words sting me just like they had when I was that teenage girl caught off guard by poisonous words of a relative. It was as if God was on the balcony with me and I heard deep in my gut brain Him saying to me that all of my life I have run away from any type of anything that would give me too much prosperity. He showed me all of the opportunities that He had given to me that I had walked away from for some outlandish reason that I had given to other people offering dumb excuses for why I couldn't go any further than what I was going. He showed me my mental block of feeling so undeserving for accomplishing the best and for always settling for good enough, because all I wanted was not to become an alcoholic drug addict with a house full of kids that turn into a lesbian and be poor for the rest of my life. You see due to that horrible seed that was planted in my mind at such a young age by my relative I thought I must have been a bad person who didn't deserve to be prosperous.

I said this simple prayer: I see the error of my ways of denying You, Oh God, full expression through me due to the fear that took up residence in me. I submit myself to You, Father, and I invite You to express Yourself fully through me so that Your people can see You in me. I evict fear, poverty, self-sabotage, and the undeserving spirit right here and right now commanding that it leaves and that it never return! Your plans, Your visions, Your kingdom, Your ways, Your time, Your success, Your love, Your tender mercies, Your gifts, Your protection, Your peace! I thank You for waiting patiently on me and keeping the hedge of protection around me in spite of me I choose You, Father, and I repent for Your kingdom is at hand! In Jesus name it is so!

Immediately I began to feel better about myself and about life with God as my Guide my self-esteem shot through the roof of knowing that I am one with the One! He began to teach me about prosperity and the levels of deservability. He explained to me that according to my faith be it unto me Matthew 9:29 (KJV). I began to believe that good was coming to me and that I deserved to have all of the desires of my heart, because God was the One that was putting the desires in my heart and who was I to deny God the opportunity to have the desires that He was giving to me stay buried inside of me! I wanted the gifts and the Giver of the gifts! I had the Giver living inside of me so quite natural the gifts would be given to me if only I believed I deserved what I was being prompted to ask for. After all Matthew 7:11(KJV) teaches if ye then, being evil, know how to give good gifts unto your children, how much more shall your Father which is in heaven give good things to them that ask him?

Ridding myself of those deep down fearful thoughts that had held me back for so many years gave me relief and freedom like I had never felt before. I was free from the power of someone else's ugly words! I was on my way to changing my circumstances and ultimately my life, because I deserve!!! I felt alive! I felt joyful! I felt excited! The chains were broken off of my life and I'd been set free to live a more vibrant, prosperous, rewarding life demonstrating God's love!

Surely, prosperity is what you make of it you can elect to run from it or embrace it so that you can operate from the overflow and I thank God for loving me enough to wait for me to become mature enough to receive what He had placed into my heart. God who is no respecter of persons according to Acts 10:34 (KJV). Knowing that God did this for me is assurance for you that He will do this for you, too; because You Deserve to enjoy life's prosperity as this is a beautiful world that you were born into so why not enjoy it!

8

Love is a many splendor thing of intense feelings of extremely deep affection. Love is a powerful unseen force of nature that can either make a person do wrong or make a person do right according to the lyrics of Albert L. Greene in his famous melody of Love and Happiness. Love is a much talked about emotion that is always on the minds and in the hearts of people regardless of race, creed, or color. 1 Corinthians 13 (KJV) has this to say about the all-powerful emotion of love:

Though I speak with the tongues of men and of angels, and have not love, I am become as sounding brass, or a tinkling cymbal. And though I have the gift of prophecy, and understand all mysteries, and all knowledge; and though I have all faith so that I could remove mountains, and have not love, I am nothing. And though I bestow all my goods to feed the poor, and though I give my body to be burned, and have not love, it profiteth me nothing. Love suffereth long, and is kind; love envieth not; love vaunteth not itself, is not puffed up, doth not behave itself unseemly, seeketh not her own, is not easily provoked, thinketh no evil; Rejoiceth not in iniquity, but rejoiceth in the truth; Beareth all things, believeth all things, hopeth all things, endureth all things. Love never faileth: but whether there be prophecies, they shall fail; whether there be tongues, they shall cease; whether there be knowledge, it shall vanish away. For we know in part, and we prophesy in part. But when that which is perfect is come, then that which is in part shall be done away. When I was a child, I spake as a child, I understood as a child, I thought as a child: but when I became a man, I put away childish things. For now we see through a glass darkly, but then face to face: now I know in part; but then shall I know even as also I am known. And now abideth faith, hope, love these three; but the greatest of these is love.

Wow! Love is an emotion that everyone at some point in their lives feel and experience and it is a beautiful thing! Love is wonderful stuff especially when what or whom you love loves you back! Love is magnificent! Love is the greatest of faith and hope and you have nothing if you have not loved! Love is spectacular! Love is to be enjoyed, shared, wanted, desired, given and received. The invisible force of love is extraordinarily amazing and you should be so in love with life that you wake up in the morning blowing God kisses as you deep breathe and stretch your way into each new day. We serve a no limit Creator of this magnificent Universe and He wants us to experience a no limit love life!

When I discovered the incredible power of love and how thinking and speaking this emotion was making me feel wonderful inside I began to say I love you to people, things, places all of the time. I began going on "love drives" where I would drive down the streets of my city and send love vibes out to everyone driving in their cars as I passed them and they passed me. If people were walking, skateboarding, riding bikes, catching the bus it didn't matter I was saying out loud "Oh, God send them love". If someone had a down trodden look on their face I would ask for extra love to go to him or her and for God to meet them at their needs. Once, I wrote "love you" to what I considered to be a childhood friend that I had known from elementary school on Facebook and later I found out he took it to mean that I was in love with him! Yuk 10 times! I'm not in love with you, but as another spirit being living in an earthly body I love you. When I found out his interpretation of my words I asked God what was I to do regarding the situation and the answer I received from the God within me was for me to keep doing what I was doing and allow people to receive whatever they feel they need to receive by the words I say or don't say and that obviously he must have needed someone to be "in love" with him at that point in his life. So I ignored the situation and continued on my love journey. I'd wake up in the morning telling life how I loved it and during the day life would show me how it loved me in return. I'd tell the Cerdidium Desert Museum tree outside of my bedroom window and balcony that I loved it for the oxygen it gave me and the beautiful yellow flowers it produces during the spring that were so aromatic and the bees that came to collect it's sweet nectar, and the humming birds that also came to collect the nectar of the yellow flowers as they always demonstrated their amazing flying and hovering abilities. I was telling complete strangers that I loved some aspect about them such as one day while I was at work the Universe saw fit to have a young lady be placed with me as part of her on the job training experience with this particular company I was working for some years ago. She was wearing false eye lashes that was decorated with rhine-stones and as I unconsciously stared at her lashes trying to picture how I would look wearing those lashes and thinking to myself that the rhinestones looked very heavy and that her eyelids were going to bulk up and build muscles and as I was picturing how her eye lids were going to look being muscular I noticed she was looking at me as if she wanted to say "lady, what are you staring at" and immediately I said "I love your lashes" she smiled and said I'll give you the name of the salon and the girl that put them on for me and she added that the salon had reasonable prices and that I'd look cute with the lashes even if I didn't get the embellishments. My neighbor always had corny jokes that he enjoyed sharing with anyone that would give him their time and ear and as I was taking out the trash he was taking out the trash and of course proceeded to ask if I had a minute for a "funny" which is what he called his jokes. I told him I had only a minute so he proceeded to tell me his joke which was so funny that I don't even remember the joke, but I laughed on que with him and then added "I love your mind" not expecting that response from me he said "thanks, neighbor,

I appreciate you" and stood watching me as I walked back into my residence. I began to love how much telling other people that I loved something about them regardless of if it was their shoes, jokes, embellished eye lashes, inanimate objects, trees, hummingbirds, whatever it didn't matter, because only love can conquer hate and 1st Corinthians have already taught us that out of faith, hope, and love that love is the greatest of the three! Thank God for love as I was operating in love on a complete different level and love began to operate in me on a complete different level!

Everyone is capable of immense love if we would simply stop putting a ceiling on the amount of love you are capable of giving and receiving. There should never be a glass ceiling on your possibilities of love or anything else and we must stop acting as if we have reached the top of the ladder of our love journey and reach out to love life! Break through the glass ceiling and love unconditionally that is love without conditions! Stop loving people for what they can do for you or for what you can get from them or for their talents, for their superficial abilities. Love like there will not be a tomorrow! Your every fiber is made of love in spite of what you have been conditioned to think and believe by the world's point of view of more sorrow and hate in the world than love. I'm here to tell you that we are made of love! Everyone needs to be loved and everybody should be loved! You should always be generous with your love, because when you share love it will come back to you in increased amounts and the more love you give the more love you will receive. Please don't pervert this and turn this into something sexual, because that is not what I'm talking about so whatever you do don't get the message twisted! John 3:16 (KJV) informs us that God so loved the world, that He gave His only begotten Son, that whosoever believeth in Him should not perish, but have everlasting life. God loved the world so much that he gave his only begotten son! Love is a never ending cycle of wonderful emotions and positive feelings and You Deserve to experience this now and always. You can never give too much love and love is never exhausted. There is no limited supply of love and if it is it is limited in your own mind. Rejoice in your love even if you share your love with someone that do not reciprocate your love then love them anyway from a distance by sending them love vibrations from your inner being.

As you fall in love with life, the Universe, God, Infinite Being, Ancient of Days, Jehova, Source or whatever name you want to call the Infinite, Limitless, Creator of all things will magnetize love back to you in wonderful creative ways. Without effort on your part you will magnetize excellent health, amazing happiness, success surpassing your wildest dreams, prosperity beyond measure and unconditional love or better stated love without conditions on your life's journey! Matthew 6:33 (KJV) But seek ye first the kingdom of God, and his righteousness; and all these things shall be added unto you You Deserve it!

Remember when I began my love journey I would go for what I called "love drives". I would get in my car and drive for an hour throughout my city sending out love vibes to all of the other drivers in other cars, people in homes, apartments, buildings of all sorts, people standing catching the bus, people riding on bikes, joggers and all passerby's that were out and about living their lives. I would go into stores and allow others with fewer items to get in front of me in line. I would give compliments to people to make their day. I would find something positive to say to every person that I came in close contact with that day with the intentions of sending good vibrations to the other person. I changed how I interacted with my family members and became more loving, respectful, kind, and courteous always offering a soft word. I held doors open for people as a kind gesture. I purchased lunch for others when they least expected it. I smiled! I relaxed! I loved!

I watched how people reacted to me as well. People appeared nicer than usual as I began to reap the love seeds I was sowing. People purchased my breakfast unexpectantly; I received a couple of unexpected bank deposits, and found money in purses that I hadn't carried in years. Individuals I had been feuding with over what now were trivial matters became kind and gentle. Also, as the disputes dissolved themselves my aches and pains dissolved as kind thoughts and words easily saturated my mind, my heart and out of my mouth as I had become a 'love angel' as I heard one young man tell his mother that I was a 'love angel'. I had energy, new opportunities, excitement, and insatiable passion for life and to help everyone discover their own love power within themselves. I love being a giver of love and I'm immensely enjoying the love that is given to me in return! This is what I want for all of you to do and that is to fall in love with life and watch and see how much life will fall in love with you! Realize the loving beauty in everything and everybody and as you hear only loving words coming from everyone including the dull and the ignorant for they too have their story is what the Desiderata taught us, speak only loving words to everyone, go to places you love to visit, watch for cars you would love to own, go to restaurants that you love eating at, shop at department stores you love to frequent, do things that you love to do and be amazed at how only loving beautiful situations began to manifest for you. If something does not fit into your love agenda then discard it from your activity list, discard it out of your sight, and out of your mind and replace it with something you love that brings you joy and happiness. Desiderata continues its instructions to us by telling us to avoid loud and aggressive people for they are vexatious to the spirit and I'm advising that you choose this day how you will feel and take control over the power of love that is yours for the taking and for the having and do not allow anyone to come between you and your love walk! You Deserve to enjoy love!

I baptize you my brother and sister in the name of the Father, the Son, and the Holy Ghost to love and to be loved this day and everyday in Jesus name! Hallelujah!!!

Now that you are a born again love person when you walk into a room your love presence will be felt as people will begin to notice a higher vibrational frequency emitting from you even though they may not realize exactly what it is that they are feeling coming from you, but they will notice something different, something better, something attractive about you that they have not noticed before.

I was in an auto body shop to get my car serviced and as I stood at the counter a man kept walking near me then walking away. This man would come and stand next to me in my personal space close enough to have our arms touching and then quickly turn and walk towards the door as if he was going to exit the building. I didn't know what the problem was and remained calm and talking to the man on the other side of the counter that was explaining the service I would need and the cost of that service. Again, the man would walk up next to me touch his arm to my arm and walk away. Making sure he wasn't pick pocketing my purse I place it on the counter in front of me. He came back and the store clerk asked him if he needed help as I looked at the man standing next to me and smiled and again he would walk away. The store clerk apologized for the bizarre behavior of this person. After about three or four times of him doing the same thing without saying a word just acting fidgety and annoyed he finally asked me if I practiced yoga. I smiled and told him that I was not a yoga practitioner. He looked confused and again he walked away to the door then back to where I was standing and the man behind the counter again spoke up asking him if there was a problem. He said when I get next to her I feel this heat and peace coming from her and I don't know what this is. He told that when he walked across the room to stand he felt the heat and peace radiating from me and the closer he'd get to me the stronger the heat would get. He said I know this sounds weird, but even when he would go outside into the heat it was a different heat and he said he could only think that I must do yoga or that I wasn't a real person so he would touch our arms to be sure. He said "I don't know why she is making me calm down when I want to be mad!" I looked at him and at the man behind the counter who was witnessing this bizarre behavior along with me and I replied "oh, that is not me per se that is the love of God in me. It's not me that you are feeling and sensing it is the loving presence of God that resides on the inside of me". That man looked at me and said "I knew it was something" and left out of the auto body store. The man behind the counter apologized to me for the scene that had just took place in their establishment. Truly what he was feeling emanating from me was the power of God that I had allowed to Divinely work through me as Revelation 3:20 (KJV) says Behold, I stand at the door, and knock: if any man hear my voice, and open the door, I will come in to him, and will sup with him, and he with me. Remember back when I told you I surrendered myself unto God.

I mentioned that someone had referred to me as a love angel well the situation that brought that on without my knowledge or me doing something specific is I picked my uncle up from the airport and he asked me to give his friend and her teenage son a ride, also. Between the time they got into my vehicle and the time I dropped them off her teenage son only said hello to me and never said another mumbling word until I dropped them off at their destination and then he said "thanks" and waved good bye as he got out of my vehicle. Two weeks later I saw the lady at an outdoor event being held by a well-known local organization and she came up to me to speak and hug my neck and she said "my son asked me if you were a love angel" and from that day to this day I refer to myself as a Love Angel. You see you don't have to say anything to people to convince them of who or what you are Luke 6:43 – 45 (KJV) says for a good tree bringeth not forth corrupt fruit; neither doth a corrupt tree bring forth good fruit. For every tree is known by his own fruit. For of thorns men do not gather figs, nor of a bramble bush gather they grapes. A good man out of the good treasure of his heart bringeth forth that which is good; and an evil man out of the evil treasure of his heart bringeth forth that which is evil for the abundance of the heart his mouth speaketh. I did not have to say one word about God or the love of God to a teenage boy, his mother, or the man at the auto body shop but the presence of God that resides on the inside of me spoke to them even if they didn't understand what they were experiencing. The mother of this teenage boy said she was shocked and surprised that on a short car ride on a warm summer's day that this was his impression of me and that he felt different being in my car. Now she was also in the car and so was my uncle, but the car ride didn't affect them the same way it affected the teenager partially because their receptive mode was on a different frequency than the receptive mode of the teenage boy. Maybe it was his innocence that caused his reception to be heightened to perceive the presence of something bigger than we were. But what I do know is that I didn't have to say one word about God or the love of God to a man in an auto body shop or to a teenage boy sitting in the back of my vehicle but the presence of God that resides on the inside of me spoke volumes to them. In the auto body shop I stood talking to a man behind the counter regarding the service I wanted to receive for my car and I was giving a ride to three people from the airport and God's presence shone through me to them. The love of God conquers all!

Make it your business to talk about the things you love to the people you love and the people you meet. Tell them all of the things you love about them. Turn your marriage around by telling your spouse all of the wonderful things that you love about him or her and don't make the things that they don't do your focus. Tell your children how you love it when they clean up their rooms without you yelling for them to clean up their rooms. Tell your supervisor how you love how efficient the office is run. Tell the mail person how you love how nice and neat s/he puts your mail in the mailbox. Tell people what you love about them and do not mention a word about what you don't love about them and see how they begin to do more things that will make you love them even more.

Begin to love life! Love the flowers, the bees that pollinate the flowers. Love the trees and the pine cones that fall from the trees. Love the smell of fresh mown grass and the fact that summer is still here. Love the snowflakes of winter and the odd shaped snow man that the neighbor's kids made that has more dirt on it than snow. Love to exercise and how beautiful you look in your birthday suite and in your clothes as a result of your dedication to your body's ability to move and perform at a level of physical fitness that enhances your overall well-being. Love your job/career and the paycheck that you receive as a result of working diligently at your job/career.

Seek out the things you love and you will find that the things you love will seek you out in return. Be aware of your surroundings. Notice the things that the Universe is allowing into your life: the smells, the colors, the insects, the traffic lights, the distant conversations that you over hear, the clouds, the rain fall, the traffic pattern, the promptings, the intuition, the taste of foods, the sound of laughter, the songs on the radio. Pay attention! Be alert! Take time to feel the vibrations of life! Don't allow your mind to have a conversation without you! Pay attention to your thoughts and your feelings ~ your love life depends on it! Control the conversations in your head instead of allowing the conversations in your head to control you. Think love thoughts! Send out love vibrations to the Universe and be amazed at how the Universe responds.

Begin to be grateful for the amount of love you are able to give and to share. Don't concern yourself with who is returning what you are giving just give what you are capable of giving and the Creator will allow you to reap the love gifts you have sown. Psalm 138 (KJV) I will praise thee with my whole heart: before the gods will I sing praise unto thee. I will worship toward thy holy temple, and praise thy name for thy lovingkindness and for thy truth: for thou has magnified thy word above all thy name. In the day when I cried thou answeredest me, and strengthenedest me with strength in my soul. All the kings of the earth shall praise thee, O Lord, when they hear the words of thy mouth. Yea, they shall sing in the ways of the Lord: for great is the glory of the Lord. Though the Lord be high, yet hath he respect unto the lowly: but the proud he knoweth afar off. Though I walk in the midst of trouble, thou wilt revive me: thou shalt stretch forth thine hand against the wrath of mine enemies, and thy right hand shall save me. The Lord will perfect that which concerneth me: thy mercy, O Lord, endureth forever: forsake not the works of thine own hands.

The more gratitude you express the more love you express. Gratitude elevates your ability to love and your ability to love increases your chances to express gratefulness. As you give thanks for the new auto, the new house, the new dress, the ability to recall an event, the job promotion, the new healthy grandchild, a prodigal son returning home, a vacation, a pod of dolphins breaching as you stand on the sand of the Atlantic Ocean, a child's first words, the perfect shoes, a friend's wedding, hey you name it it's up to you just simply know you are giving love! Every time you express gratitude you are expressing love.

I once heard Frederick K.C. Price say that his prayers to God was simply "God, I thank you for all things!" then he looked at the congregation and asked "what is left out of all" looking around he answered his own question and said "nothing, because all is an all-inclusive term". At the time I was young and spiritually immature yet receptive to the teachings of God to enhance my life and I thought how arrogant is that, but at the same time I knew he was on to something and over the years I would ponder "what is left out of all" and occasionally I would say "God, I thank you for all things" and keep doing whatever it was that I was doing at the moment knowing that nothing was left out of all. I knew what I learned from the Apostle had some validity to it, but I didn't know just how much validity it was. Then the answer came to me some thirty years later that showing gratitude magnetizes more of what you are giving thanks for back to you.

I learned over the years that being definite and on purpose was a more structured way of showing gratitude which is ultimately showing love. So being grateful for the money means I had ushered more money to me. Being grateful for the good positive relationships in my life brought more good and positive relationships to me. Being grateful for the 1,600 square feet townhouse caused me to be able to upgrade to a newer larger 2,800 square feet home in which to live. Being grateful for the weekend getaway brought a two week holiday to me and then I was asked to go on a three month vacation with Parisian friends that the Universe had allowed me to become meet via our daughter's becoming friends by being teammates on a gymnastics team. At the time I was asked about the 3 month vacation I wasn't there mentally and I asked if it was normal for people to vacation for 3 months and I remember thinking how something had to be wrong with being able to vacation for 3 months! Now, I think like the Parisians thought back then in terms of everyone is supposed to go on 3 month vacations whenever they desire to do so. I have evolved! Then I heard Shawn C. Carter mention about being on a permanent vacation with a shiny new beach chair and then suddenly I realized with God all things are possible that He (God) meets us at our level of consciousness. All that I showed love towards by offering up loving gratitude multiplied back to me far beyond what I had imagined each time!

I had love and gratitude coming from my every pore. I loved showing love. I loved being loved and I looked forward to being thankful and grateful for all that I loved! This was an awesome never ending cycle for me and I thanked God that I had finally understood what the Apostle was trying to tell me almost thirty years before. I was grateful for everything I had received in my life! I was grateful for everything I was receiving in my life! I was grateful for all that I wanted to experience in my life as if I had already received the desire which is a directive of Romans 4:17 (KJV) (As it is written, I have made thee a father of many nation,) before him whom he believed, even God, who quickeneth the dead, and calleth those things which be not as though they were! What?! God called those things which be not as though they were! All you have to do is act like you know!

I changed my life by simply living in a loving mindset and being grateful to God and all that He does! When I gave thanks every now and again I received back abundance from the Universe every now and again. When I gave love and gratitude continuously I received back from the Universe continuously. I was reaping what I was sowing. I was receiving what I was giving. I was getting less negativity and more positivity on a daily basis. My intention was to be definite and on purpose in my love walk! God is love! I am love! Regardless of what negative situation or circumstance that would try to find a way into my life I would find something positive about the situation and love the lesson I was learning or that this life situation was teaching and the next thing I would know is that the tables had turned in my favor. I love life and so should you as every negative situation was turning out to be for my good as it is written in Genesis 50:20 (KJV) but as for you, ye thought evil against me; but God meant it unto good, to bring to pass, as it is this day, to save much people alive.

Regardless of the situation I found myself in I would find something to be grateful for and so should you. Don't contemplate the negative focus on the positive and if you have lemons make lemonade and be grateful for those lemons that was given to you so that you could make the lemonade. When something good happens during your day give thanks to the Creator for allowing that goodness to touch your life. I began to give thanks for green lights, parking spaces, songs on the radio, flashes of good memories, my food digesting easily, my clothes fitting nicely, my bad hair days that caused me to be creative in coming up with new hairstyles, if I sent a text and received no response from the intended receiver of the text I gave God thanks just as if I had received a response back from the receiver.

Understanding that love and gratitude are collaborators I began giving love and thanks for everything: my eyes, my sense of touch, my knee caps, my toenails, my veins, my internal city that operates inside my body on a daily and nightly basis, my autoimmune system (because on the inside of each of our bodies is an entire world all of its own and of great proportions that go unnoticed until a rogue cell goes amok), garbage disposals, the thread of my car tires, everything!

I recommend that you, too, send love and gratitude to every cell, organ, tissue, bone, fiber, hair follicle all the way down to the macular level of your body that is created in the image of the Creator Genesis 1:27 (KJV) so God created man in his own image, in the image of God created he him; male and female created he them and Psalm 139:14 (KJV) I will praise thee; for I am fearfully and wonderfully made: marvelous are thy works; and that my soul knoweth right well. Love this and thank God for this, because it is a wonderful and marvelous gift to us as spirits to be encapsulated in such amazing earth suites!

Give love and be grateful always, because love and gratitude enhances you with all of the riches of life, because love and gratitude multiplies back to you what you have sown and you reap what you sow: Galatians 6:7 – 9 (KJV) Be not deceived; God is not mocked: for whatsoever a man soweth, that shall he also reap. For he that soweth to his flesh shall of the flesh reap corruption; but he that soweth to the Spirit shall of the Spirit reap life everlasting. And let us not be weary in well doing: for in due season we shall reap, if we faint not. You Deserve!

Now get creative and begin to come up with ways you can give love and show gratitude and come into full harmony with our loving Father by being in the spirit of earnest love and gratitude for the blessings you have received (past); the blessings you currently have (present), and the blessings you call as though you already have by being definite and on purpose (future) and remember Matthew 22:36 – 40 (KJV) Master, which is the great commandment in the law? Jesus said unto him, Thou shalt love the Lord thy God with ALL thy heart, and with ALL thy soul, and with ALL thy mind. This is the first and great commandment. And the second is like unto it. Thou shalt love thy neighbor as thyself. On these two commandments hang ALL the law and the prophets and above ALL things have fervent love among yourselves: for love shall cover a multitude of sins 1 Peter 4:8. And like Fred K.C. Price once said "what's left out of ALL?"

9

My Definite Purpose:

My definite purpose for writing this book is that you elevate your life to the next level by unlocking the secrets that are dormant deep within you. As you step out of your past and into your future my desire is that you tap into that deep reservoir of your soul and allow the rivers of Living Water to flow forth from you to give life to all that you meet on your journey in order that you may help others on their journey in this game called life. Know that You Deserve the best that life has to offer now go ahead and be free and keep in mind that I've not told you anything that you don't already have knowledge of I'm just initiating the activation of your dormant gifts that lay inside of you waiting for the chance to be set free! Because that which has been is what will be, that which is done is what will be done, and there is nothing new under the sun Ecclesiastes 1:9 (KJV). Use the following scriptures to strengthen your faith, prayer life, prosperity, health, healing, protection, love, joy, patience, peace, the ability to overcome, and gratitude to help keep you elevated as you reside always in the promises of God (all scripture versus are from KJV):

The Power of Faith

Having faith makes it possible to receive anything from God. Make sure your faith is strong by practicing it always: believe, confess (act), and receive.

Joshua 1:8 This book of the law shall not depart out of thy mouth; but thou shalt meditate therein day and night, that thou mayest observe to do according to all that is written therein: for then thou shalt make thy way prosperous, and then thou shalt have good success.

Psalm 62:8 Trust in him at all times; ye people, pou4r out your heart before him: God is a refuge for us. Selah.

Psalm 35:5 Commit thy way unto the LORD; trust also in him; and he shall bring it to pass.

Hebrews 10:35, 36 Cast not away therefore your confidence, which hath great recompence of reward. For ye have need of patience, that, after ye have done the will of God, ye might receive the promise.

Galatians 6:9 And let us not be weary in well doing: for in due season we shall reap, if we faint not.

Hebrews 11:6 But without faith it is impossible to please him: for he that cometh to God must believe that he is, and that he is a rewarder of them that diligently seek him.

Hebrews 11:1 Now faith is the substance of things hoped for, the evidence of things not seen.

I John 5:14, 15 And this is the confidence that we have in him, that, if we ask anything according to his will, he heareth us: And if we know that he hear us, whatsoever we ask, we know that we have the petitions that we desired of him.

James 1:5 – 8 If any of you lack wisdom, let him ask of God, that giveth to all men liberally, and upbraideth not; and it shall be given him. But let him ask in faith, nothing wavering. For he that wavereth is like a wave of the sea driven with the wind and tossed. For let not that man think that he shall receive anything of the Lord. A double minded man is unstable in all his ways.

Romans 12:3 For I say, through the grace given unto me, to every man that is among you, not to think of himself more highly than he ought to think; but to think soberly, according as God hath dealt to every man the measure of faith.

Romans 1:17 For therein is the righteousness of God revealed from faith to faith: as it is written, The just shall live by faith.

The Power of Prayer

Prayer is communicating with God simply having a rapport with Him interchanging thoughts or feelings to Him. It can be a time of praise and worship. It can be time spent interceding on someone else's behalf or it can be petitioning God to meet a specific need. Whatever the reason, season, or occasion there is power in prayer!

I Peter 3:12 For the eyes of the Lord are over the righteous, and his ears are open unto their prayers: but the face of the Lord is against them that do evil.

John 15:7 If ye abide in me, and my words abide in you, ye shall ask what ye will, and it shall be done unto you.

James 5:16 Confess your faults one to another, and pray one for another, that ye may be healed. The effectual fervent prayer of a righteous man availeth much.

John 16:23 And in that day ye shall ask me nothing. Verily, verily, I say unto you, whatsoever ye shall ask the Father in my name, he will give it to you.

Matthew 18:19 Again I say unto you, that if two of you shall agree on earth as touching anything that they shall ask, it shall be done for them of my Father which is in heaven.

Psalm 66:18 – 20 If I regard iniquity in my heart, the Lord will not hear me: but verily God hath heard me; he hath attended to the voice of my prayer. Blessed be God, which hath not turned away my prayer, nor his mercy from me.

Psalm 102:17 He will regard the prayer of the destitute, and not despise their prayer.

Psalm 100:4, 5 Enter into his gates with thanksgiving, and into his courts with praise: be thankful unto him, and bless his name. for the Lord is good; his mercy is everlasting; and his truth endureth to all generations.

Hebrews 7:25 Wherefore he is able also to save them to the uttermost that come unto God by him, seeing he ever liveth to make intercessions for them.

Psalm 37:4 Delight thyself also in the Lord: and he shall give thee the desires of thine heart.

Proverbs 15:8 The sacrifice of the wicked is an abomination to the Lord: but the prayer of the upright is his delight.

God's Prosperity, Health, Healing, and Protection

Deuteronomy 8:18 But thou shalt remember the Lord thy God: for it is he that giveth thee power to get wealth, that he may establish his covenant which he sware unto thy fathers, as it is this day.

Psalm 34:9 O fear the Lord, he his saints: for there is no want to them that fear him.

Isaiah 55:11 So shall my word be that goeth forth out of my mouth: it shall not return unto me void, but it shall accomplish that which I please, and it shall prosper in the thing whereto I sent it.

Malachi 3:10 Bring ye all the tithes into the storehouse, that there may be meat in mine house, and prove me now herewith, saith the Lord of hosts, if I will not open you the windows of heaven and pour you out a blessing, that there shall not be room enough to receive it.

Luke 6:38 Give, and it shall be given unto you; good measure, pressed down, and shaken together, and running over, shall men give into your bosom. For with the same measure that ye mete withal it shall be measured to you again.

Proverbs 3:9, 10 Honor the Lord with thy substance, and with the firstfruits of all thine increase: so shall thy barns be filled with plenty, and thy presses shall burst out with new wine.

Psalm 34:10 The young lions do lack, and suffer hunger: but they that seek the Lord shall not want any good thing.

Matthew 6:33 But seek ye first the kingdom of God, and his righteousness; and all these things shall be added unto you.

II Corinthians 9:6, 7 But this I say, He which soweth sparingly shall reap also sparingly; and he which soweth bountifully shall reap also bountifully. Every man according as he purposeth in his heart, so let him give; not grudgingly, or of necessity: for God loveth a cheerful giver.

Exodus 15:26 And said, If thou wilt diligently hearken to the voice of the Lord thy God, and wilt do that which is right in his sight, and wilt give ear to his commandments, and keep all his statutes, I will put none of these diseases upon thee, which I have brought upon the Egyptians: for I am the Lord that healeth thee.

I Peter 2:24 Who his own self bare our sins in his own body on the tree, that we, being dead to sins, should live unto righteousness: by whose stripes ye were healed.

Galatians 3:13, 14 Christ hath redeemed us from the curse of the law, being made a curse for us: for it is written cursed is every one that hangeth on a tree: That the blessing of Abraham might come on the Gentiles through Jesus Christ; that we might receive the promise of the Spirit through faith.

III John 1:2 Beloved, I wish above all things that thou mayest prosper and be in health, even as thy soul prospereth.

Proverbs 4:20 – 22 My son, attend to my words; incline thine ear unto my sayings. Let them not depart from thine eyes; keep them in the midst of thine heart. For they are life unto those that find them, and health to all their flesh.

I John 3:21, 22 Beloved, if our heart condemn us not, then have we confidence toward God. And whatsoever we ask, we receive of him, because we keep his commandments, and do those things that are pleasing in his sight.

Psalm 91:1, 2 & 5, 6 He that dwelleth in the secret place of the most High shall abide under the shadow of the Almighty. I will say of the Lord, He is my refuge and my fortress: my God; in Him will I trust. Thou shalt not be afraid for the terror by night; nor for the arrow that flieth by day; nor for the pestilence that walketh in darkness; nor for the destruction that wasteth at noonday.

Psalm 34:7 The angel of the Lord encampeth round about them that fear him, and delivereth them.

Psalm 27:5 For in the time of trouble he shall hide me in his pavilion: in the secret of his tabernacle shall he hide me; he shall set me up upon a rock.

Isaiah 54:14, 15, 17 In righteousness shalt thou be established: thou shalt be far from oppression; for thou shalt not fear: and from terror; for it shall not come near thee. Behold, they shall surely gather together, but not by me: whosoever shall gather together against thee shall fall for thy sake. No weapon that is formed against thee shall prosper; and every tongue that shall rise against thee in judgement thou shalt condemn. This is he heritage of the servants of the Lord, and their righteousness is of me, saith the Lord.

Psalm 105, 14, 15 He suffered no man to do them wrong: yea, he reproved kings for their sakes; saying touch not mine anointed and do my prophets no harm.

The Fruit of Love, Joy, Patience, and Peace

John 3:16 For God so loved the world, that he gave His only begotten Son, that whosoever believeth in him should not perish, but have everlasting life.

I John 4:18, 19 There is no fear in love; but perfect love casteth out fear: because fear hath torment. He that feareth is not made perfect in love. We love him, because he first loved us.

I John 4:7, 8 Beloved, let us love one another: for love is of God; and every one that loveth is born of God, and knoweth God. He that loveth not knoweth not God; for God is love.

John 13:34, 35 A new commandment I give unto you, That ye love one another; as I have loved you, that ye also love one another. By this shall all men know that ye are my disciples, if ye have love one to another.

Romans 8:38, 39 For I am persuaded, that neither death nor life, nor angels, nor principalities, nor powers, nor things present, nor things to come, nor height, nor depth, nor any other creature, shall be able to separate us from the love of God, which is in Christ Jesus our Lord.

I Corinthians 13:1 – 7 Though I speak with the tongues of men and of angels, and have not love, I am become as sounding brass or a tinkling cymbal. And though I have the gift of prophecy, and understand all mysteries, and all knowledge; and though I have all faith, so that I could remove mountains, and have not love, I am nothing. And though I bestow all my goods to feed the poor, and though I give my body to be burned, and have not love, it profiteth me nothing. Love suffereth long, and is kind; love envieth not; love vaunteth not itself, is not puffed up, doth not behave itself unseemly, seeketh not her own, is not easily provoked, thinketh no evil; rejoiceth not in iniquity, but rejoiceth in the truth; beareth all things, believeth all things, hopeth all things, endureth all things.

Matthew 25:23 His lord said unto him, well done, good and faithful servant; thou hast been faithful over a few things, I will make thee ruler over many things: enter thou into the joy of the lord.

Jeremiah 15:16 Thy words were found, and I did eat them; and thy word was unto me the joy and rejoicing of mine heart: for I am called by thy name, O Lord God of hosts.

James 1:2, 3 My brethren, count it all joy when ye fall into divers temptations; knowing this, that the trying of your faith worketh patience.

I Peter 4:12, 13 Beloved, think it not strange concerning the fiery trial which is to try you, as though some strange thing happened unto you: but rejoice, inasmuch as ye are partakers of Christ's sufferings; that, when his glory shall be revealed, ye may be glad also with exceeding joy.

Psalm 35:27 Let them shout for joy, and be glad, that favor my righteous cause: yea, let them say continually, Let the Lord be magnified, which hath pleasure in the prosperity of his servant.

Isaiah 26:3 Thou wilt keep him in perfect peace, whose mind is stayed on thee: because he trusteth in thee.

Isaiah 32:17 And the work of righteousness shall be peace; and the effect of righteousness quietness and assurance forever.

John 14:27 Peace I leave with you, my peace I give unto you: not as the world giveth, give I unto you. Let not your heart be troubled, neither let it be afraid.

John 16:33 These things I have spoken unto you, that in me ye might have peace. In the world ye shall have tribulation: but be of good cheer; I have overcome the world.

Proverbs 16:7 When a man's ways please the Lord, he maketh even his enemies to be at peace with him.

II Corinthians 13:11 Be perfect, be of good comfort, be of one mind, live in peace; and the God of love and peace shall be with you.

Philippians 4:6, 7 Be careful for nothing; but in everything by prayer and supplication with thanksgiving let your requests be made known unto God. And the peace of God, which passeth all understanding, shall keep your hearts and minds through Christ Jesus.

Hebrews 10:35, 36 Cast not away therefore your confidence, which hath great recompence of reward. For ye have need of patience, that, after ye have done the will of God, ye might receive the promise.

II Peter 1:4 – 7 whereby are given unto us exceeding great and precious promises: that by these ye might be partakers of the divine nature, having escaped the corruption that is in the world through lust. And beside this, giving all diligence, add to your faith virtue; and to virtue knowledge; and to knowledge temperance; and to temperance patience; and to patience godliness; and to godliness brotherly kindness; and to brotherly kindness love.

Romans 5:3 – 5 And not only so, but we glory in tribulations also: knowing that tribulation worketh patience; and patience, experience; and experience, hope: and hope maketh not ashamed; because the love of God is shed abroad in our hearts by the Holy Ghost which is given unto us.

I Timothy 6:11, 12 But thou, O man of God, flee these things; and follow after righteousness, godliness, faith, love, patience, meekness. Fight the good fight of faith, lay hold on eternal life, whereunto thou art also called, and hast professed a good profession before many witnesses.

Isaiah 26:3 Thou wilt keep him in perfect peace, whose mind is stayed on thee: because he trusteth in thee.

John 14:27 Peace I leave with you, my peace I give unto you: not as the world giveth, give I unto you. Let not your heart be troubled, neither let it be afraid.

Romans 5:1, 2 therefore, being justified by faith, we have peace with God through our Lord, Jesus Christ: By whom also we have access by faith into this grace wherein we stand, and rejoice in hope of the glory of God.

Ability to Overcome

Temptations, test, trials, alcohol, overeating, heartache, fear, worry, procrastinations, emptiness, sexual immorality, strife, jealousy, doubt, unbelief, gossiping, back biting, restlessness, frustrations, drug abuse, and all other ills of life can be overcome by the grace of God!

Jeremiah 17:7, 8 Blesses is the man that trusteth in the Lord, and whose hope the Lord is. For he shall be as a tree planted by the waters, and that spreadeth out her roots by the river, and shall not see when heat cometh, but her leaf shall be green; and shall not be careful in the year of drought, neither shall cease from yielding fruit.

Psalm 91:4 – 7 He shall cover thee with his feathers, and under his wings shalt thou trust: his truth shall be thy shield and buckler. Thou shalt not be afraid for the terror by night; nor for the arrow that flieth by day; nor for the pestilence that walketh in darkness; nor for the destruction that wasteth at noonday. A thousand shall fall at thy side, and ten thousand at thy right hand; but is shall not come nigh thee.

Isaiah 43:2 When thou passest through the waters, I will be with thee; and through the rivers, they shall not overflow thee: when thou walkest through the fire, thou shalt not be burned; neither shall the flame kindle upon thee.

Isaiah 54:17 No weapon that is formed against thee shall prosper; and every tongue that shall rise against thee in judgment thou shalt condemn. This is the heritage of the servants of the Lord, and their righteousness is of me, saith the Lord.

Proverbs 3:5,6 Trust in the Lord with all thine heart; and lean not unto thine own understanding. In all thy ways acknowledge him, and he shall direct thy paths.

Psalm 18:1 – 3 I will love thee, O Lord, my strength. The Lord is my rock, and my fortress, and my deliverer; my God, my strength, in whom I will trust; my buckler, and the horn of my salvation, and my high tower. I will call upon the Lord, who is worthy to be praised: so shall I be saved from mine enemies.

Joshua 1:8 This book of the law shall not depart out of thy mouth; but thou shalt meditate therein day and night, that thou mayest observe to do according to all that is written therein: for then thou shalt make thy way prosperous, and then thou shalt have good success.

Psalm 103:10, 12 He hath not dealt with us after our sins; nor rewarded us according to our iniquities. As far as the east is from the west, so far hath he removed our transgressions from us.

I Corinthians 3:16 Know ye not that ye are the temple of God, and that the Spirit of God dwelleth in you?

Romans 8:1, 2 There is therefore now no condemnation to them which are in Christ, Jesus, who walk not after the flesh, but after the Spirit. For the law of the Spirit of life in Christ Jesus hath made me free from the law of sin and death.

Philippians 3:13, 14 Brethren, I count not myself to have apprehended: but this one thing I do, forgetting those things which are behind, and reaching forth unto those things which are before, I press toward the mark for the prize of the high calling of God in Christ Jesus.

Galatians 5:24, 25 And they that are Christ's have crucified the flesh with the affections and lusts. If we live in the Spirit, let us also walk in the Spirit.

Romans 12:1, 2 I beseech you therefore, brethren, by the mercies of God, that ye present your bodies a living sacrifice, holy, acceptable unto God, which is your reasonable service. And be not conformed to this world: but be ye transformed by the renewing of your mind, that ye may prove what is that good, and acceptable, and perfect, will of God.

Hebrews 2:18 For in that he himself hath suffered being tempted, he is able to succor them that are tempted.

Jeremiah 33:3 Call unto me, and I will answer thee, and show thee great and mighty things, which thou knowest not.

Psalm 139:23, 24 Search me, O God, and know my heart: try me, and know my thoughts: and see if there be any wicket way in me, and lead me in the way everlasting.

Psalm 124:8 Our help is in the name of the Lord, who made heaven and earth.

Psalm 23:4 Yea, though I walk through the valley of the shadow of death, I will fear no evil: for thou art with me; thy rod and thy staff they comfort me.

Luke 12:32 Fear not, little flock; for it is your Father's good pleasure to give you the kingdom.

Psalm 27:1 The Lord is my light and my salvation; whom shall I fear? the Lord is the strength of my life; of whom shall I be afraid?

Isaiah 41:10 Fear thou not; for I am with thee; be not dismayed; for I am thy God: I will strengthen thee; yea, I will help thee; yea, I will uphold thee with the right hand of my righteousness.

Psalm 138:7 Though I walk in the midst of trouble, thou wilt revive me: thou shalt stretch forth thine hand against the wrath of mine enemies, and thy right hand shall save me.

Isaiah 40:31 But they that wait upon the Lord shall renew their strength; they shall mount up with wings as eagles; they shall run, and not be weary; and they shall walk, and not faint.

Psalm 112:7 He shall not be afraid of evil tidings: his heart is fixed, trusting in the Lord.

Luke 10:19 Behold, I give unto you power to tread on serpents and scorpions, and over all the power of the enemy: and nothing shall by any means hurt you.

John 10:10 The thief cometh not, but for to steal, and to kill, and to destroy: I am come that they might have life, and that they might have it more abundantly.

Psalm 55:22 Cast thy burden upon the Lord, and he shall sustain thee: he shall never suffer the righteous to be moved.

Romans 8:31 What shall we then say to these things? If God be for us, who can be against us?

Joshua 1:9 Have not I commanded thee? Be strong and of a good courage; be not afraid, neither be thou dismayed: for the Lord thy God is with thee whithersoever thou goest.

I John 5:4 For whatsoever is born of God overcometh the world: and this is the victory that overcometh the world, even our faith.

Psalm 34:15, 17, 19 The eyes of the Lord are upon the righteous, and his ears are open unto their cry. The righteous cry, and the Lord heareth, and delivereth them out of all their troubles. Many are the afflictions of the righteous: but the Lord delivereth him out of them all.

Psalm 37:23, 24 The steps of a good man are ordered by the Lord: and he delighteth in his way. Though he fall, he shall not be utterly cast down: for the Lord upholdeth him with his hand.

Matthew 11:28 – 30 Come unto me, all ye that labor and are heavy laden, and I will give you rest. Take my yoke upon you, and learn of me; for I am meek and lowly in heart: and ye shall find rest unto your souls. For my yoke is easy, and my burden is light.

Romans 14:23 And he that doubteth is damned if he eat, because he eateth not of faith: for whatsoever is not of faith is sin.

Hebrews 10:23 – 25 Let us hold fast the profession of our faith without wavering; (for he is faithful that promised;) And let us consider one another to provoke unto love and to good works: not forsaking the assembling of ourselves together, as the manner of some is; but exhorting one another: and so much the more, as ye see the day approaching.

Proverbs 6:4 – 10 Give not sleep to thine eyes, nor slumber to thine eyelids. Deliver thyself as a roe from the hand of the hunter, and as a bird from the hand of the fowler. Go to the ant, thou sluggard; consider her ways, and be wise: which having no guide, overseer, or ruler, provideth her meat in the summer, and gathereth her food in the harvest. How long wilt thou sleep, O sluggard? When wilt thou arise out of they sleep? Yet a little sleep, a little slumber, a little folding of the hands to sleep: so shall thy poverty come as one that travelleth, and thy want as an armed man.

James 4:8 Draw nigh to God, and he will draw nigh to you. Cleanse your hands, ye sinners; and purify your hearts, ye double minded.

Matthew 7:1, 2 Judge not, that ye be not judged. For with what judgment ye judge, ye shall be judged: and with what measure ye mete, it shall be measured to you again.

Matthew 7:4, 5 Or how wilt thou say to thy brother, let me pull out the mote out of thine eye; and, behold, a beam is in thine own eye? Thou hypocrite, first cast out the beam out of thine own eye; and then shalt thou see clearly to cast out the mote out of thy brother's eye.

Acts 17:24 – 28 God that made the world and all things therein, seeing that he is Lord of heaven and earth, dwelleth not in temples made with hands; neither is worshipped with men's hands, as though he needed anything, seeing he giveth to all life, and breath, and all things; and hath made of one blood all nations of men for to dwell on all the face of the earth, and hath determined the times before appointed, and the bounds of their habitation; that they should seek the Lord, if haply they might feel after him, and find him, though he be not far from every one of us: for in him we live, and move, and have our being; as certain also of your own poets have said, for we are also his offspring.

John 13:34, 35 A new commandment I give unto you, that ye love one another; as I have loved you, that ye also love one another. By this shall all men know that ye are my disciples, if ye have love one to another.

Psalm 121:1 – 3 I will lift up mine eyes unto the hills, from whence cometh my help. My help cometh from the Lord, which made heaven and earth. He will not suffer thy foot to be moved: he that keepeth thee will not slumber.

Isaiah 54:4, 5 I will lift up mine eyes unto the hills, from whence cometh my help. My help cometh from the Lord, which made heaven and earth. He will not suffer thy foot to be moved: he that keepeth thee will not slumber.

Romans 8:38, 39 For I am persuaded, that neither death, nor life, nor angels, nor principalities, nor powers, nor things present, nor things to come nor height, nor depth, nor any other creature, shall be able to separate us from the love of God, which is in Christ Jesus our Lord.

Proverbs 6:32 But whoso committeth adultery with a woman lacketh understanding: he that doeth it destroyeth his own soul.

I Corinthians 6:19, 20 What know ye not that your body is the temple of the Holy Ghost which is in you, which ye have of God, and ye are not your own? For ye are bought with a price: therefore glorify God in your body, and in your spirit, which are God's.

II Corinthians 5:10 For we must all appear before the judgment seat of Christ; that every one may receive the things done in his body, according to that he hath done, whether it be good or bad.

James 4:7 Submit yourselves therefore to God. Resist the devil, and he will flee from you.

I John 5:18 We know that whosoever is born of God sinneth not; but he that is begotten of God keepeth himself, and that wicked one toucheth him not.

I Corinthians 6:9, 10 Know ye not that the unrighteous shall not inherit the kingdom of God? Be not deceived: neither fornicators, nor idolaters, nor adulterers, nor effeminate, nor abusers of themselves with mankind, nor thieves, nor covetous, nor drunkards, nor revilers, nor extortioners, shall inherit the kingdom of God.

I John 1:9 If we confess our sins, he is faithful and just to forgive us our sins, and to cleanse us from all unrighteousness.

I Thessalonians 4:3, 4 For this is the will of God, even your sanctification, that ye should abstain from fornication: that every one of you should know how to possess his vessel in sanctification and honor; not in the lust of concupiscence, even as the Gentiles which know not God: that no man go beyond and defraud his brother in any matter: because that the Lord is the avenger of all such, as we also have forewarned you and testified.

Galatians 6:8 For he that soweth to his flesh shall of the flesh reap corruption; but he that soweth to the Spirit shall of the Spirit reap life everlasting.

Romans 13:13, 14 Let us walk honestly, as in the day; not in rioting and drunkenness, not in chambering and wantonness, not in strife and envying. But put ye on the Lord Jesus Christ, and make not provisions for the flesh, to fulfil the lusts thereof.

Proverbs 3:30 Strive not with a man without cause, if he have done thee no harm.

Galatians 5:19 – 21 Now the works of the flesh are manifest, which are these; adultery, fornication, uncleanness, lasciviousness, idolatry, witchcraft, hatred, variance, emulations, wrath, strife, seditions, heresies, envyings, murders, drunkenness, revellings, and such like: of the which I tell you before, as I have also told you in time past, that they which do such things shall not inherit the kingdom of God.

II Timothy 2:23 But foolish and unlearned questions avoid, knowing that they do gender strifes.

Romans 8:1 – 4, 6 There is therefore now no condemnation to them which are in Christ Jesus, who walk not after the flesh, but after the Spirit. For the law of the Spirit of life in Christ Jesus hath made me free from the law of sin and death. For what the law could not do, in that it was weak through the flesh, God sending His own Son in the likeness of sinful flesh, and for sin, condemned sin in the flesh: that the righteousness of the law might be fulfilled in us, who walk not after the flesh, but after the Spirit. For to be carnally minded is death; but to be spiritually minded is life and peace.

II Corinthians 10:3 – 5 For though we walk in the flesh, we do not war after the flesh: (for the weapons of our warfare are not carnal, but mighty through God to the pulling down of strong holds;) casting down imaginations, and every high thing that exalteth itself against the knowledge of God, and bringing into captivity every thought to the obedience of Christ;

James 1:5 – 8 If any of you lack wisdom, let him ask of God, that giveth to all men liberally, and upbraideth not; and it shall be given him. But let him ask in faith, nothing wavering. For he that wavereth is like a wave of the sea driven with the wind and tossed. For let not that man think that he shall receive anything of the Lord. A double minded man is unstable in all his ways.

Romans 4:20, 21 He staggered not at the promise of God through unbelief; but was strong in faith, giving glory to God; and being fully persuaded that, what he had promised, he was able also to perform.

Mark 9:23 Jesus said unto him, if thou canst believe, all things are possible to him that believeth.

Philippians 4:8 Finally, brethren, whatsoever things are true, whatsoever things are honest, whatsoever things are just, whatsoever things are pure, whatsoever things are lovely, whatsoever things are of good report; if there be any virtue, and if there be any praise, think on these things.

James 4:7 Submit yourselves therefore to God.

I John 4:4 Ye are of God, little children, and have over-come them: because greater is He that is in you, than he that is in the world.

Matthew 12:36, 37 But I say unto you, that every idle word that men shall speak, they shall give account thereof in the day of judgment. For by thy words thou shalt be justified, and by thy words thou shalt be condemned.

Ephesians 4:29 – 32 Let no corrupt communication proceed out of your mouth, but that which is good to the use of edifying, that it may minister grace unto the hearers. And grieve not the holy Spirit of God, whereby ye are sealed unto the day of redemption. Let all bitterness, and wrath, and anger, and clamor, and evil speaking, be put away from you, with all malice: and be ye kind one to another, tenderhearted, forgiving one another, even as God for Christ's sake hath forgiven you.

Job 27:3, 4 All the while my breath is in me, and the spirit of God is in my nostrils; my lips shall not speak wickedness, or my tongue utter deceit.

James 3:10 Out of the same mouth proceedeth blessing and cursing. My brethren, these things ought not so to be.

James 1:26 If any man among you seem to be religious, and bridleth not his tongue, but deceiveth his own heart; this man's religion is vain.

I Peter 3:10, 11 For he that will love life, and see good days, let him refrain his tongue from evil, and his lips that they speak no guile: let him eschew evil, and do good; let him seek peace, and ensue it.

Luke 6:45 A good man out of the good treasure of his heart bringeth forth that which is good; and an evil man out of the evil treasure of his heart bringeth forth that which is evil: for of the abundance of the heart his mouth speaketh.

Colossians 4:6 Let your speech be always with grace, seasoned with salt, that ye may know how ye ought to answer every man.

Psalm 91:11 For he shall give his angels charge over thee, to keep thee in all thy ways.

John 8:31, 32 Then said Jesus to those Jews which believed on him, if ye continue in my word, then are ye my disciples indeed; and ye shall know the truth, and the truth shall make you free.

Psalm 127:2 It is vain for you to rise up early, to sit up late, to eat the bread of sorrows: for so he giveth his beloved sleep.

Hebrews 13:5 Let your conversation be without covetousness; and be content with such things as ye have: for he hath said, I will never leave thee, nor forsake thee.

Confessions of Gratitude

Galatians 3:14 Thank You, god, that the blessing of Abraham might come on the Gentiles through Jesus Christ; that we might receive the promise of the Spirit through faith.

II Corinthians 9:6 – 8 Thank You, God, I sow bountifully, therefore, I reap bountifully. God, You have made all grace about toward me. I, having all sufficiency of all things, do abound to every good work.

Luke 6:38 Thank You, God, I have given and it is given unto me good measure, pressed down, shaken together, and running over shall men give into my bosom.

Galatians 1:4 Thank You, God, I am delivered from the evils of the present world because it is the will of You, God, concerning me.

I Corinthians 1:30 Thank You, God, Jesus is my Lord and He is my wisdom, righteousness, sanctification and redemption. Therefore, I am free from ignorance.

Colossians 2:10 Thank You, God, I am complete in You who is the head of all principality and power.

I John 5:14, 15 Thank You, God, this is the confidence that I have in God. The word declares that if I ask anything according to Your will, Father, that You hear me, and if I know that You hear me, I have the petitions that I desire of You.

Matthew 6:33 Thank You, God, all the blessings of Yours are mine, for I seek first the kingdom of God and Your righteousness.

Hebrews 10:23 Thank You, God, I hold fast the confessions of my faith without wavering, because I know You are faithful to keep Your promises.

Philippians 4:6, 7 Thank You, God, I am not anxious about anything, but in everything by prayer and supplication with thanksgiving I let my requests be made known unto You, oh God, and Your peace which passes all understanding keeps my heart and mind at peace through Christ, Jesus.

Mark 16:17, 18 Thank You, God, I am a believer and these signs do follow me. In the name of Jesus I cast out demons, I speak with new tongues, I lay hands on the sick and they do recover.

I Corinthians 15:58 Thank You, God, I stand steadfast, unmoveable, always abounding in the work of the Lord, because I know my labor is not in vain in the Lord.

Romans 12:1, 2 Thank You, God, I present my body a living sacrifice holy, acceptable unto God, and I am not conformed to this world, but I am renewed in my mind daily that I may prove what is that good, and acceptable, and perfect will of You, God, for my life.

Ephesians 4:29 – 31 Thank You, God, I let no corrupt communications come out of my mouth, and I grieve not the Holy Spirit. I put away all bitterness and wrath, and anger and evil speaking.

Luke 10:19 Thank You, God, I have the authority to walk on Satan and his demons and over all the power of the enemy and nothing by any means shall harm me.

Philippians 3:10, 14 Thank You, God, I forget those things which are behind and I reach forth unto those things which are before, I press toward the mark for the prize of the high calling of God in Christ.

Romans 8:1, 2 Thank You, God, there is no condemnation to me because I walk not after the flesh, but after the Spirit; for the law of the Spirit of life in Christ Jesus had made me free from the law of sin and death.

Romans 8:38, 39 Thank You, God, neither death, nor life, nor angels, nor principalities, nor powers, nor things present nor things to come, nor height, nor depth, nor any other creature can separate me from the love of You, God, which is in Christ Jesus.

Colossians 1:13 Thank You, God, I have been delivered from the power of darkness, and I have been translated into the kingdom of Jesus Christ. Satan has no dominion over me.

II Timothy 1:7 Thank You, God, I have not been given a spirit of fear, but of power, love, and a sound mind.

I Peter 2:24 Thank You, God, Jesus bore my sins in His own body on the tree that I being dead to sins, should live unto righteousness by whose stripes I am healed.

II Corinthians 3:17 Thank You, God, I am free from bondage for where the Spirit of the Lord is, there is liberty.

I peter 5:7 Thank You, God, I am free from worry for I am to cast my cares upon You.

I John 1:7 Thank You, God, I am free from sin, for the blood of Jesus Christ cleanseth me from all sin.

Mark 12:30, 31 Thank You, God, I love You Lord with all my heart, with all my soul, with all my mind, and with all my strength: this is the first commandment and the second is like, namely this. I shalt love my neighbor as myself. There is none other commandment greater than these.

Thank You, God, now I am the master of my thoughts.

Thank You, God, life is so easy and good as all good things come to me now.

Thank You, God, I am healthy, happy, successful, prosperous, and loved.

Thank You, God, I am experiencing all of the joy that I love.

Thank You, God, I give gifts of love continuously.

Thank You, God, all of my actions and desires are supported by Cosmic Intelligence.

Thank You, God, I am doing and being all that my heart desires to do and be.

Thank You, God, I live in a world of abundance, happiness, and joy.

Thank You, God, I have a wonderful prosperous business in wonderful prosperous ways, and I give wonderful prosperous service for wonderful prosperous pay.

Thank You, God, money comes to me in increasing amounts through multiple sources on a continuous basis.

Thank You, God, I am choosing my thoughts carefully and wisely which is dictating my speech to be careful and wise.

Thank You, God, I am a masterful creator of my own life by masterfully selecting my thoughts.

Thank You, God, I live in a no limit universe serving a no limit God.

Thank You, God, I ask, I believe, and I receive.

Thank You, God, I seek Your Kingdom and Your righteousness first.

Thank You, God, I am a citizen of Your Kingdom.

Thank You, God, I delight myself in Your laws.

Thank You, God, I have faith in You and in Your Word taking Your Word on trust.

Thank You, God, I am the image and likeness of You.

Thank You, God, I am eternally Yours.

Thank You, God, for the beauty of the flowers, trees, oceans, mountains, sun, moon, and stars.

Thank You, God, money is forever circulating freely in my life and there is always a Divine surplus.

Thank You, God, I am advancing, I am growing, I am moving forward financially, emotionally, spiritually as I am continuously seeking Your Kingdom and Your righteousness.

Thank You, God, I am mastering and managing my money according to Your guidance and Your wisdom of earthly things.

Thank You, God, for my wisdom and spiritual discernment as I help others as on their life journey as Your Spirit guides and directs me.

Thank You, God, I am love and You love me unconditionally.

Thank You, God, I am eternally prosperous in every area of my life.

Thank You, God, I am on the right path which is Your path.

Thank You, God, I am skillful, talented, and well able to follow Your promptings.

Thank You, God, my sleep is always peaceful.

Thank You, God, You are my source.

Thank You, God, I walk in the consciousness of Your presence and Your fullness flows through me always filling me up and over flowing with the goodness of Your Kingdom and Your righteousness.

Thank You, God, my financial accounts and investments portfolios are overflowing with abundance, increase, and prosperity.

Thank You, God, I am leaving a financial and spiritual inheritance for my children and their children.

Thank You, God, I am living in a global community and infect Your children with Your loving kindness and tender mercies as they see through me and see You.

Thank You, God, abundance is Your will for my life.

Thank You, God, Your love covers a multitude of sin.

Thank You, God, in my own person and practice I am demonstrating the way to affluence so that I may be able to influence per Your guidance and instruction.

Thank You, God, that You hear me.

Thank You, God, I live in the now.

Thank You, God, I am experiencing life to its fullest every day in every way.

Thank You God, I now have perfect work in a perfect way and I give perfect service for perfect pay.

God I give You thanks in the magnanimous name of Jesus Christ of Nazareth for the opportunity to write this book!

You Deserve…

Health,

Happiness,

Success,

Prosperity,

&

Love!

Joan has a Bachelor of Science in Psychology degree with a specialty in Industrial Organization Psychology. She is a graduate student attending Capella University Harold Abel School of Psychology Master's program with intentions on pursuing a Doctoral in Psychology. She has studied metaphysical causes of illnesses combined with Biological Psychology, Addiction Theories, Massage Therapy, Respiratory Therapy, and Arterial Blood Gasses. She is a current member of The Foundation for the Advancement of Social Theory Research Project, and she host the following two blogs in her spare time: http:// perfectways.blogspot.com and https://lovinglifeblogcast.blogspot.com. Most importantly she says she is an avid student of The Holy Bible!